One Word From God Can Change Your Finances

By Kenneth and Gloria Copeland

Harrison House
Tulsa, Oklahoma

One Word From God Can Change Your Finances

30-0709

07 06 05 04 03 02 01 00   10 9 8 7 6 5 4 3

All Scripture is from the *King James Version* unless otherwise noted as the following:

The Amplified Bible, Old Testament copyright © 1965, 1987 by The Zondervan Corporation. *The Amplified New Testament* copyright © 1958, 1987 by The Lockman Foundation. Used by permission.

New King James Version, copyright © 1982 by Thomas Nelson, Inc.

The Holy Bible, New International Version, copyright © 1973, 1978, 1884 by the International Bible Society. Used by permission of Zondervan Publishing House.

New American Standard Bible®, copyright © 1960, 1962, 1963, 1968, 1971, 1972, 1973, 1975, 1977, 1994 by the Lockman Foundation. Used by permission.

New Testament in Modern English, J.B. Phillips, copyright © J.B. Phillips 1958, 1959, 1960, 1972.

The Living Bible, copyright © 1971. Used by permission of Tyndale House Publishers Inc., Wheaton, Illinois 60189. All rights reserved.

One Word From God Can Change Your Finances
ISBN 1-57794-146-2
Copyright © 1999 by Kenneth and Gloria Copeland
Kenneth Copeland Ministries
Fort Worth, Texas 76192-0001

Published by Harrison House, Inc.
P.O. Box 35035
Tulsa, Oklahoma 74153

Contents

Introduction

One Word From God Can Change Your Life FOREVER!

When the revelation of this statement exploded on the inside of me, it changed the way I think...about everything! I had been praying for several days about a situation that seemed at the time to be overwhelming. I had been confessing the Word of God over it, but that Word had begun to come out of my head and not my heart. I was pushing in my flesh for the circumstance to change. As I made my confession one more time, the Spirit of God seemed to say to me, *Why don't you be quiet?!*

I said, "But Lord, I'm confessing the Word!"

He answered inside me, *I know it. I heard you. Now just be still and be quiet a little while, and let the Word of God settle down in your spirit. Quit trying to make this thing happen. You're not God.*

You're not going to be the one to make it happen anyway!

So I stopped. I stopped in that situation in my mind and began to get quiet before the Lord...and this phrase came up in my spirit..."**One word from God can change anything.**"

So I started saying that. I said it off and on all day. It came easily because it came from God—not from my own thinking.

Every time I was tempted to worry or think of ideas concerning my circumstances, I'd think, *Yes, just one word from God...*

I noticed when I'd say that, **the peace of God** would come on me. It was so calming. As a result, a habit developed in me. People would bring me issues. They'd say, "Well, what about..." And I'd either say aloud or think to myself, "**Yeah, that may be so, but one word from God will change anything.**"

It began to be the answer for everything. If I was watching television and the newscaster was telling about a disaster, and the people being interviewed were saying things to the effect of "Oh, what are we going to do. It's all been blown away, burned up or shook up...," I'd say, **"Yeah, but one word from God can change anything."**

It really developed into a strength for me and it can for you. That's why we've put together the **One Word From God Book Series**...there could be just one word in these inspiring articles that can change your finances forever.

You've been searching, seeking help...and God has the answer. He has the one word that can turn your circumstance around and put you on dry ground. He has the one word that gives you all the peace that's in Him. He is your Father. God wants you to be blessed so that you can be a blessing. He wants to open the windows of heaven and pour you out a blessing so there is not room enough to receive it. (Malachi 3:12)

God loves you. And He has a word for you. One Word that can change your life FOREVER!

Kenneth Copeland

Breaking the Power of Debt

Chapter 1

"If the Son therefore shall make you free, ye shall be free indeed."
— JOHN 8:36

John Avanzini

A strong sense of hopelessness...That is the way many Christians describe their inner feelings about their finances. They feel as if they are aimlessly adrift in an endless stream of borrowing. Unpaid bills occupy more and more of their thoughts. They honestly believe there is no way out of their debt dilemma.

Please note that I am not speaking of dishonest people, but hardworking, honest folks who are doing all they know to do. However, try as they may, they keep sliding further and further into debt.

The Joy Is Gone

In most homes, both husband and wife are forced to work. Yet, even with two wage earners, money always seems to be in scarce supply.

For most families, the joy is gone from payday. All that remains is the Friday night ritual of rushing the paycheck to the bank so the checks they wrote Thursday will not bounce. After the paycheck is deposited, they draw out a few dollars from the automatic teller machine for their once-a-week, Friday night splurge. This consists of a modest meal at a fast food restaurant and a short walk through the mall. Long gone are the days of shopping, for they must now pay for their past credit sprees.

For a pitiful few hours, the wage earner feels good, enjoying a small portion of the fruit of his labor. All too soon Saturday morning arrives, and with it comes the full reality of the fruit of debt. The wage earner must now face his mountain of bills—bills that were only partially paid last payday.

God Is Left Holding the Bag

Check after check is written until, finally, the last pressing obligation is paid. With this task accomplished, the stark reality comes to light. There is only enough left to barely scrape by until next payday.

In the crushing pressure of having only enough to make ends meet, the tithe, which is so vital to receiving God's blessings in life, is usually ignored. At best only a portion of it is paid. This is usually justified with a promise that soon things will be better and then God will get what is His.

For the next six days, the average wage earner has to put off having any fun or doing anything special. To the Christian, the most painful part of this existence is having to say no to God concerning giving into His kingdom. This is an empty cycle that is routinely made from Friday to Friday by those who have come under the control of the spirit of debt.

Wake Up to a Better Way!

Wake up! That's no way for the children of God to live! Surely this is not God's best for your life! He must have a better plan. Deep down in your spirit, you know

He wants something more for your life than barely existing from payday to payday!

Hear the good news! The same God Who wants you to walk in His saving grace, the same God Who wants you to experience His miracle healing power, the same God Who wants your family to be entirely whole also wants you to operate in total financial abundance.

His principles of biblical economics are clearly stated in His Word! If you follow them, they will free you of your payday-to-payday blues. From them you will learn how to boldly get started on your road to a debt-free lifestyle.

A Progressive Walk

God is as concerned about your financial success as He is about every other part of your life.

When you first started to walk with Him, you had to learn to recognize the lies of the devil. They were holding you captive. The world had taught you that drinking and parties were the fun way to live. But as you progressed in your Christian walk, you realized that that kind of thinking is flawed. You began to understand that drinking almost always leads to alcoholism and wild parties open the door to sexual sins. You found that if you were to experience God's best, you would have to say no to sin and yes to God's way of doing things.

The further you walked in God's ways, the less complicated your world became. Inner peace began to grow. Much to your own surprise, you started having more fun instead of less fun. Since the troubles and torments that accompany the world's wicked ways have begun to melt away, your life has become much more worthwhile.

Well, Child of God, I've got good news for you. This same freedom that you are experiencing in this area of your life is also available to you in your finances!

Please do not misunderstand. I'm not talking about something that will force you into the lifestyle of a miser. I'm talking about something that will enable you to experience a miracle in your finances—a miracle that will transform your finances from barely making it to abundance, from not enough to more than enough, from little to much.

Does such a miracle exist? Can we actually go forward in some financial healing line, have someone lay hands on us, and walk away with all of our bills marked paid in full?

Before I answer that question, let us get one thing straight. No man has the ability to miraculously release people from their debts. Miracles are not from men. Miracles are given by God and received, through faith, by men.

I have laid hands on many people and seen them healed; however, I have never healed anyone. Each time someone has been miraculously healed, that person had to receive the miracle from God.

The same biblical principle applies to the miraculous release from debt. Each time the miracle of debt cancellation takes place, it comes directly from God to those who receive it through faith.

A Widow Received This Miracle

Make no mistake about it. The miracle of canceled debt is taught in God's Word. One very powerful illustration involves a widow woman and her two sons.

This widow was left with a great debt at her husband's death. She was hopelessly bound until the miracle of debt cancellation set her free. Her debt was so large that her two sons were sentenced to become bond servants to the creditor. It took everything she had. She was left with nothing more than a small pot of oil. She was brought to the very door of destitution. In her advanced years, she was cruelly sentenced to the life of a beggar.

Thank God for her faith. Her decision not to seek help from the creditor proved to be the wisest move of her life. In the midst of her desperate problem, she turned to her man of God. All the creditor could offer her was more debt, but God presented her with the opportunity to receive the miracle of canceled debt. All she had to do was exercise the faith to do exactly what her man of God told her to do.

The following verses tell us about her powerful miracle of debt cancellation:

> Now there cried a certain woman ...unto Elisha, saying, Thy servant my husband is dead...and the creditor is come to take unto him my two sons to be bondmen. And Elisha said unto her...what hast thou in the house? And she said...a pot of oil. Then he said, Go, borrow thee vessels...And when thou art come in, thou shalt...pour out into all those vessels, and thou shalt set aside that which is full...And it came to pass, when the vessels were full...the oil stayed. Then she came and told the man of God. And he said, Go, sell the oil, and pay thy debt... (2 Kings 4:1-7).

There it is, right from the pages of your own Bible! A miraculous cancellation of debt! The scriptural account of this particular event opened with an impossible mountain of debt. It demanded payment. Even if it meant the ruination of the woman and her two sons, it had to be paid. Then, in just a few hours, this woman was completely debt free!

With this miracle from God's Word, we see proof positive that He has a miraculous solution for the debt problems of people just like you and me. What we need to do is dig into the Bible and find it, then mix it with faith and put it to work in our lives.

Chapter 2

Build Your Financial Foundation

Gloria Copeland

"Beloved, I wish above all things that thou mayest prosper and be in health, even as thy soul prospereth."

— 3 JOHN 2

Never try to build a house without first laying a foundation.

I don't care how eager you are to get it finished, how excited you are about filling it with furniture and decorating it all just right—take the time to put down a solid foundation first. If you don't, that house will be so unstable it will soon come tumbling down.

That's simple advice, isn't it? Everyone with any sense at all knows it. Yet in the spiritual realm, people make that mistake all the time. They see a blessing God has promised them in His Word, and they are so eager to have it, they ignore the foundational basics of godly living and pursue just that one thing.

That's especially true in the area of prosperity. Often, people are so desperate for a quick financial fix, they just pull a few prosperity promises out of the Bible and try to believe them—without allowing God to change anything else in their lives. Of course, it doesn't work and those people end up disappointed. Sometimes they even come to the conclusion that it wasn't God's will for them to prosper after all.

But I can tell you today, from the Word of God and from personal experience: It is definitely God's will for all of His children to prosper!

That's why He inspired the Apostle John to write, *"Beloved, I wish above all things that thou mayest prosper and be in health, even as thy soul prospereth"* (3 John 2).

Notice there, however, that John didn't just say, "I want you to prosper." He said, "I want you to prosper as your soul prospers." He tied financial prosperity to the prosperity of our mind, will and emotions.

God's plan is for us to grow financially as we grow spiritually. He knows it is dangerous to put great wealth into the hands of someone who is too spiritually immature to handle it. You can see dramatic evidence of that fact in the lives of people who have acquired financial riches through this world's system, apart from God. In most cases, such riches just help people to die younger and in more misery than they would have if they'd been poorer.

That's because they use their wealth to sin in greater measure. They use it to buy all the cocaine they want and drink all the alcohol they want. They use it to pay for an immoral lifestyle that eventually destroys them.

The wages of sin is death. That is an inescapable fact. So, when people get money and use it to sin, it does them more harm than good. As Proverbs 1:32 says, *"The prosperity of fools shall destroy them."*

Seek First Things First

In light of that truth, it's easy to see why God wants us to increase financially at the same rate we increase spiritually. He wants us to outgrow our fleshly foolishness so our prosperity will bring us blessing and not harm.

"But Gloria," you say, "I need financial help fast!"

Then get busy growing. Get busy building your foundation for prosperity.

How? By finding out what God says in His Word and doing it.

You see, the foundation of prosperity is a continual lifestyle built on the Word of God. It is doing whatever God tells you to do, thinking whatever He tells you to think, and saying whatever He tells you to say.

Godly prosperity is the result of putting God's Word—all of it, not just the parts about financial prosperity—first place in your life. It comes when you apply His principles on a continual basis—not just because you want money, but because Jesus is your Lord and you want to follow Him. It comes when you start obeying the instructions Jesus gave us in Matthew 6:25-33:

I tell you, stop being perpetually uneasy (anxious and worried) about your life, what you shall eat or what you shall drink, and about your body, what you shall put on. Is not life greater [in quality] than food, and the body [far above and more excellent] than clothing? Look at the birds of the air; they neither sow nor reap nor gather into barns, and yet your heavenly Father keeps feeding them. Are you not worth more than they? And which of you by worrying and being anxious can add one unit of measure [cubit] to his stature or to the span of his life? And why should you be anxious about clothes? Consider the lilies of the field and learn thoroughly how they grow; they neither toil nor spin; Yet I tell you, even Solomon in all his magnificence (excellence, dignity and grace) was not arrayed like one of these.

But if God so clothes the grass of the field, which today is alive and green and tomorrow is tossed into the furnace, will He not much more surely clothe you, O you men with little faith? Therefore do not worry and be anxious, saying, What are we going to have to eat? or, What are we going to have to drink? or What are we going to have to wear? For the Gentiles (heathen) wish for and crave and diligently seek after all these things; and your heavenly Father well knows that you need them all. But seek for (aim at and strive after) first of all His kingdom, and His righteousness [His way of doing and being right], and then all these things taken together will be given you besides *(The Amplified Bible)*.

I remember back before Ken and I knew we could trust God to take care of us financially, I thought it was my job to worry about how we were going to pay our bills. I spent a great deal of my time thinking things like, *What am I going to do about this light bill? How am I going to keep the electricity from being shut off?* To me it would have been irresponsible not to worry about such things!

Then I found out it wasn't God's will for me to worry. It was His will for us to believe Him to care for us. I also learned that as believers, we're not to seek after material riches. We're not to pursue money like people do who are without God. They have to pursue it. They don't have a covenant with God, so if they don't seek material goods, they won't get them!

But we're not like those people. We're not in the world without God and without a covenant (Ephesians 4:12-13). We have God's promise of provision. He has assured us in His Word that He will not only meet our needs, but give us an abundance.

It's important for us to remember, however, that a covenant is always between two parties. It has two sides to it. A covenant says, If you do this, then I'll do that.

God's part of the covenant is to prosper us—spirit, soul and body as well as financially. What is our part of the covenant? It's not to seek after that prosperity. If we do that, we'll get sidetracked. Our part of the covenant is to seek first His kingdom, His way of doing and being right!

Our part is to say, "Lord, I'll do whatever You tell me to do. I'll obey Your Word and do what is right in Your sight—even if it looks like it will cost me."

Of course, obeying God's Word never costs in the long run. It pays! You always put yourself in a position for increase when you seek after God and do things His way.

I'll be honest with you though, there will be times when you can't see how that increase is going to come. Ken and I know about those times. We've been through them.

When we saw in the Word of God that we were to *"Keep out of debt and owe no man anything, except to love one another"* (Romans 13:8, *The Amplified Bible),* we weren't too excited about it. At that time in our lives, it looked to us like we'd never be able to do anything financially without borrowing money.

We thought, *How will we ever get a car? How will we get a home? How will we finance our ministry? We're doomed!*

But we had already decided to obey God no matter what the cost, so we committed to Him to get out of debt even though we thought it would be to our disadvantage. Of course, that decision has since turned out to be one of the wisest financial decisions we've ever made.

That's the way it always is. Obeying God always works to your advantage in the end!

Become a Candidate for Increase

It's easy to see how following God's instructions to get out of debt affected our prosperity. But the fact is, our decision to obey other, seemingly unrelated commands we saw in the Word also had an impact on our finances.

That's because you can't separate God's financial principles from the rest of His principles. They all work together. So you have to take the whole Bible to have a good foundation for godly prosperity.

The primary commandment Jesus gave us, for example, is to *"love one another"* (John 15:12). To the casual observer that commandment may seem to have nothing to do with money, yet to have true prosperity love must be the guiding force of your life. You must be quick to apply scriptural principles for living like these found in 1 Peter 3:8-11:

> **Finally, all [of you] should be of one and the same mind (united in spirit), sympathizing [with one another], loving [each the others] as brethren (of one household), compassionate and courteous— tenderhearted and humble-minded. Never return evil for evil or insult for insult—scolding, tonguelashing, berating; but on the contrary blessing—praying for their welfare, happiness and protection, and truly pitying and loving them.**

> **For know that to this you have been called, that you may yourselves**

inherit a blessing...For let him who wants to enjoy life and see good days...keep his tongue free from evil, and his lips from guile (treachery, deceit). Let him turn away from wickedness and shun it; and let him do right *(The Amplified Bible).*

Think of it this way. Every right action you take, every godly decision you make, every time you go love's way instead of the selfish way, you're putting another block on your foundation of prosperity.

When you pray for your enemies instead of hating them, you become a candidate for increase. When you turn away from immorality, you're turning toward blessing. When you see things in your life that you know aren't right and you correct them according to the Word of God, you're preparing yourself to handle greater financial abundance.

The book of Proverbs is full of God's wisdom about everyday things and decisions. It will help you learn how to handle your affairs in a way that is pleasing to God. And since it has 31 chapters, by reading a chapter a day along with your other Bible reading, you can finish it in just a month. It will increase you to read Proverbs over and over.

In Proverbs you'll find out, for example, that the quality of faithfulness and the blessing of prosperity are tied together very closely. Wherever you find one, you'll find the other. For as Proverbs 28:20 says, *"A faithful man shall abound with blessings."* According to Webster's dictionary, a faithful man is one who "adheres to duty, of true fidelity, loyal, true to allegiance, and constant in the performance of duties or services."

Luke 16:10 says, *"He who is faithful in a very little [thing], is faithful also in much; and he who is dishonest and unjust in a very little [thing], is dishonest and unjust also in much" (The Amplified Bible).* So if you want to be trusted with more and be promoted to a better job, be faithful and honest in the job you have right now.

You may think Christian people don't need to hear about honesty and faithfulness, but they do. I know personally of cases where Christians have stolen money from their employers.

They may not have intended to "steal" anything. They may have just thought, *Well, I'll borrow this money for a couple of weeks and then I'll put it back and no harm will be done.* The problem is, you can't borrow something from someone without their permission. That's stealing and you can't be blessed and steal.

Taking that money may have seemed all right to those people when they did it. They may have made excuses and justified it in their own minds. But if they'd been studying and obeying the Word of God, they wouldn't have fallen for those excuses. That's because the Word discerns the thoughts and intents of the heart (Hebrews 4:12). It teaches you what is right and what isn't.

It reveals not man's way, but God's way of doing and being right. It enables you to lay a firm foundation for godly prosperity.

Build the Whole House

With that foundation laid, you'll be ready to step out in faith and receive the abundance God has in store for you.

Many people who have lived godly lives have failed to do that so they've missed out on God's financial blessings. Although they've continually applied the principles of God's Word and become prime candidates for great prosperity, they've unwittingly passed it by because religious tradition has taught them that God wants them in poverty. Christians like that have great wealth in their spiritual bank account, but because they don't realize it's there, they never tap into it!

Don't let that happen to you. Don't just build the foundation for prosperity and stop there. Go on and build the whole house. Dare to believe that if you'll seek first God's kingdom, His way of doing and being right, all other things (the food, the clothes, the cars, the houses, everything!) will be added to you as well.

Build your foundation, then dare to believe—and you will surely prosper!

Money Really Matters

Chapter 3

"If you are willing and obedient,
you shall eat the good of the land."
— Isaiah 1:19,
The Amplified Bible

Gloria
Copeland

"Well, I'm not rich...But in the eternal scheme of things money doesn't really matter. Right?" Wrong. In this day and hour, financial prosperity isn't simply a luxury. It's a responsibility. For the committed believer who cares about the eternal destiny of others, money really matters.

I want to talk to you about a subject that is vital to the kingdom of God. A subject that will have a tremendous impact, not only on your life in these days but also on the lives of others.

I want to talk to you about money.

I realize you may not think money is a very spiritual issue. You may have been taught that as far as God is concerned, it doesn't matter if you're rich or poor. But I want you to know—it matters. Your not having enough money to finance the gospel won't keep you from going to heaven, but it could keep others from going.

Prosperity is not a frivolous thing with no eternal consequences. It is a serious issue. If you want to know how serious, consider this: Right now, in areas such as Eastern Europe, there are people who have never heard the gospel. For years, the doors of their nations have been locked to it. But at this moment, the Body of Christ has the opportunity to preach the Word of God from one end of that area to the other.

What will we need to take full advantage of that opportunity? Money.

That's right. Money, or the lack of it, can determine whether someone in a area like that hears the gospel...or not. In my eyes, that makes our prosperity as born-again believers an important issue—extremely important.

If we prosper, we'll have enough not just to meet our own little needs, but to send the Word of God around the world. If we don't, we won't. It's that simple.

"Oh, but Gloria, you know we can't all be rich."

Yes, we can. Prosperity is not an accident. It's not a function of circumstances or the economy. According to God's Word, prosperity is a choice. It is a personal decision and a spiritual process.

Most people don't know that. Ken and I didn't either years ago when we first began walking with God. Back then, we were sick some of the time and broke all the time. Our life was one financial disaster after another. It felt like we were living under some kind of curse.

Do you know why we felt that way? Because we were living under a curse! We just didn't realize it.

Failing to prosper is part of the curse that came upon the earth when Adam sold out to Satan in the Garden of Eden. The curse is described in detail in Deuteronomy 28:15-68 and it includes every kind of sickness, sin, tragedy and lack. That passage says that when you're living under the curse *"You shall be only oppressed and robbed continually...You shall carry much seed out into the field, and shall gather little in"* (verses 29, 38, *The Amplified Bible*).

Do you ever feel like that? Like every time you try to get ahead, something happens to steal away everything you thought you were going to gain? I know the feeling. I had it for years.

But then, one day Ken and I discovered we had been redeemed from the curse. We found out that according to the Word of God, we didn't have to put up with any of those things listed in Deuteronomy 28:15-68 because: *"Christ hath redeemed us from the curse of the law, being made a curse for us: for it is written, Cursed is every one that hangeth on a tree: That the blessing of Abraham might come on the Gentiles through Jesus Christ; that we might receive the promise of the Spirit through faith"* (Galatians 3:13-14).

Overtaken—For Better or Worse

Look at the last part of that scripture again. It says the blessing of Abraham has come on the gentiles through Christ Jesus.

I know there are many people who say God's blessings are only spiritual and they don't include finances. But that can't be true because the Bible says we have the blessing of Abraham and that blessing brought him great wealth. Genesis 24:35 makes that quite clear.

There Abraham's servant says: *"And the Lord [has] blessed my master greatly; and he is become great: and he hath given him flocks, and herds, and silver, and gold, and menservants, and maidservants, and camels, and asses."*

God had promised Abraham that He would be his shield and his exceeding great reward (Genesis 15:1). No question about it, that promise caused Abraham to be extremely prosperous in every way and it will do the same for you, if you're a born-again child of God. What is it like to be blessed in every way? (Remember blessed means empowered to prosper.) Deuteronomy 28:1-9 tells us:

> **And it shall come to pass, if thou shalt hearken diligently unto the voice of the Lord thy God, to observe and to do all his commandments**

which I command thee this day, that the Lord thy God will set thee on high above all nations of the earth: And all these blessings shall come on thee, and overtake thee, if thou shalt hearken unto the voice of the Lord thy God.

Blessed shalt thou be in the city, and blessed shalt thou be in the field. Blessed shall be the fruit of thy body, and the fruit of thy ground, and the fruit of thy cattle, the increase of thy kine, and the flocks of thy sheep. Blessed shall be thy basket and thy store. Blessed shalt thou be when thou comest in, and blessed shalt thou be when thou goest out.

The Lord shall cause thine enemies that rise up against thee to be smitten before thy face: they shall come out against thee one way, and flee before thee seven ways. The Lord shall command the blessing upon thee in thy storehouses, and in all that thou settest thine hand unto;

and he shall bless thee in the land which the Lord thy God giveth thee. The Lord shall establish thee an holy people unto himself.

Does all that sound too good to be true? Well, it's not. That's the blessing Jesus bought for you on the cross. And it will begin to operate in your life if you'll *"hearken...unto the voice of the Lord [your] God."*

Notice, I didn't say it will operate just because you're a Christian. Ken and I were Christians for five years before we began to listen to God's Word about prosperity. So during that time, the curse continued to run loose in our lives. It didn't just creep up quietly. It jumped on us and overtook us. No matter how hard we tried, we couldn't outrun it or get away from it.

Then we began to believe God's Word about prosperity—to be willing and obedient—and good things started to happen. First a few. Then a few more. The longer we obeyed God and walked in faith about finances, the more those good things increased.

Just like the curse once overtook us, now the blessings of God overtake us. I like that much better.

The same thing will happen to you if you'll follow the instructions in Deuteronomy 28:1 and *"hearken diligently unto the voice of the Lord...."* That's because *"faith cometh by hearing, and hearing by the word of God"* (Romans 10:17). Once faith comes, you can speak to that mountain of financial trouble, command it to be removed, and it will obey you. (See Mark 11:22-24.)

You must realize, however, that faith for finances doesn't come automatically. It doesn't come just because you're a good person and you love God. It comes when you spend time, day after day, listening to and acting on what God's Word says about prosperity.

More Than Enough

As you do that you'll discover, just as Ken and I did, that God doesn't promise just to meet your basic needs, He says He'll give you an abundance. Some religious people would argue about that. But the truth is, there's nothing to argue about because the Word makes it perfectly clear. Look back at what we just read from Deuteronomy 28. It says, *"The Lord shall command the blessing upon thee in thy storehouses, and in all that thou settest thine hand unto"* (verse 8).

Look at that for a minute. If you don't have abundance, why would you need a storehouse? A storehouse is where you put the extra, the surplus, the "more than enough."

If that's not clear enough, verse 11 says point-blank that, *"the Lord shall make you have a surplus of prosperity" (The Amplified Bible).* I want you to remember those words—a surplus of prosperity—because that's God's will for you. When you made Jesus Christ the Lord of your life, God's blessing came upon you not so you could just "get by," but so that you could have a surplus of prosperity!

That shouldn't really surprise you. After all, if you look at God's history with man, you'll see that when He had His way, man was abundantly supplied. Everything in the Garden of Eden, for example, was good. The temperature was just right. The food was right there on the trees. All you had to do was pull it off and eat it. Talk about fast food! Adam and Eve lacked nothing in the garden.

All through Israel's history, God supplied their every need, even if He had to bring down manna from heaven. As long as they obeyed Him and honored Him, their families prospered, their livestock prospered, their crops prospered, and no enemy could stand before them. On top of that, there was no sickness in the midst of them.

God has always promised, *"If you are willing and obedient, you shall eat the good of the land"* (Isaiah 1:19, *The Amplified Bible*). Understand, though, that being willing means more than just saying, "Well, Lord, if You want me to prosper, I'll prosper." Being willing means that you apply the force of your will and determine to receive by faith what God has promised, no matter how impossible the circumstances may seem to be.

Get Aggressive!

That's what Ken and I had to do. When we saw in God's Word that prosperity belonged to us, we were so deep in debt it looked like we would never get out. But we applied our will anyway. We said, "We will prosper in the Name of Jesus. God says He has provided abundance, so abundance belongs to us!"

That's the kind of aggressive faith you need to believe for prosperity. I didn't understand that for years so, without realizing it, I allowed the devil to come in and give me a hard time over finances. Then one day, God revealed to me that I needed to use the same kind of faith for finances I used to receive healing.

That changed my believing and my actions. You see, I had learned early on to be aggressive about healing. Once Ken and I found out that Jesus bore our sickness, we refused to put up with it anymore. We absolutely wouldn't tolerate it. We considered sickness an enemy and when it would try to come into our house, we'd stand against it.

We'd tell it, "No! You get out of here. We've been redeemed from the curse of the law and that includes every sickness and disease. So get out!"

Sure enough, it would leave. Never in all the time my children were at home did I have to take them to the doctor for sickness. (We certainly would have if it had been necessary.) They'd get symptoms now and then, but we'd just pray and believe God, and they always got healed. Sometimes it took a day or so, but the healing always came.

One day God said to me, *Why don't you treat lack that same way? Why do you put up with it? You say you've been redeemed from it, but you haven't resisted it like you do sickness and disease.*

When I heard that, I determined to make a change. I began to actively, aggressively resist lack and to cultivate my faith for prosperity as diligently as I had cultivated my faith for healing. And I can tell you, it made a big difference in our lives.

Start Where You Are

I must warn you though, it wasn't easy. It takes effort and perseverance in the Word of God to develop that kind of faith. If you want to believe for divine prosperity, you'll need to keep a constant dose of the Word of God in your heart. You'll need to meditate on it all the time.

You can't just grab a verse once in a while and then run out and prosper. You have to let the Word of God renew your mind and teach you how to think differently and you'll have to let that Word take root in your heart. That doesn't happen overnight.

I've heard people say, "Well, we've been tithing and obeying God and we're not out of debt yet. Is there any way to hurry this thing up?"

Yes. You can double up on the Word, spend more time with God, and be sure to give every time God tells you. That's in addition, of course, to tithing 10 percent of your income that belongs to God—offerings come after that. But even so, you still have to start where you are.

When Ken and I were first learning to walk in faith for prosperity, we didn't know very much of God's Word yet. We got our revelation piece by piece. Every time we'd learn something new, we'd put it into practice.

Actually, it's much easier for us now to walk in prosperity than it was back then. Today, we have to believe for millions of dollars just to pay our TV bills. But that's not nearly as challenging as it was to believe God back then for food on the table. During those days I often had to pray in the spirit just to pay my way out at the grocery store. That was the hardest time of all because we were just learning.

You have to grow in these things. If you're just now hearing that God wants you to prosper, you probably won't be able to get a million dollars in cash by this time next week.

Why? Because your faith isn't up to that yet. What you need to do is start right where you are. Start believing God for rent money. Start believing God to buy groceries. Start believing, and then increase.

That's what we did. We believed for rent. Then we believed for a car. Then one day we believed for a house. The first time it took us six years to get it. The next time it took three weeks.

We just kept growing. We kept listening to God and walking in the faith that we had and it got bigger. And we kept tithing and giving!

No Time to Waste

What's important is to start now. Don't wait until next month. Start believing God for the things you need today. Start thanking Him for them. Tell the devil you're out from under his curse. Grab hold of the Word of God and don't let go.

If you'll do that and stay with it, and continue to do what God tells you, you'll eventually have a surplus of prosperity so that you can not only pay your bills, but also have the capacity to give into every good work! (2 Corinthians 9:6-11).

So get out the Word and get busy. There's no time to waste. We're rapidly coming to the end of this age. We have opportunities today we've never had before. Nations are allowing us to preach the gospel on television that never allowed it before. But it takes money to do that.

Who's going to provide that money? You and I and every other member of the Body of Christ who will dare to rise up and reject lack as a lifestyle. Every believer who will be bold enough to say, "Prosperity belongs to me. I will believe it and I will receive it in Jesus' Name! I will stand up to the devil and fight the fight of faith for it!"

It's time we realized it's not just our own personal needs that are hanging in the balance. It's more than that. It's the eternal destiny of other people. It's the work of the kingdom of God.

Prosperity is not a frivolous matter. It's serious. More hinges on it than you have realized. So get aggressive. Take a stand on the Word of God and take what belongs to you as His child. I won't kid you, you'll have to fight some battles. But I can tell you in advance, if you'll do it in faith, you'll win. It will be well worth the fight.

Chapter 4

Prosperity— It's Not an Option

Markus Bishop

"Let them shout for joy, and be glad, that favour my righteous cause: yea, let them say continually, Let the Lord be magnified, which hath pleasure in the prosperity of his servant."
— PSALM 35:27

Have you ever noticed how sensitive people are about their money? You can talk to them about the way they look, the way they talk, even about their family. But when you start talking about their money— watch out!

Money seems to be where people really live. The truth is, they are that way about money because that's the way the devil is about money.

When you start talking about money, you really stir up the devil! You have to understand that he is the god of this world (2 Corinthians 4:4). But he is not

God of the earth. Scripture says, *"...the earth is the Lord's, and the fullness thereof"* (1 Corinthians 10:26).

The devil is the god of the world's system. When you start talking about the prosperity of believers, you are talking about money being taken out of the devil's pocket. That money comes from his operation—his kingdom—and it's put over into the kingdom of God to help pay for the gospel being preached throughout the world. That makes him mad!

Satan's Lie About God

That's why he has promoted the lie that money is evil, even though Scripture says, *"The love of money is the root of all evil"* (1 Timothy 6:10). That's why by his deception, there is some perverted preaching going on in the pulpits of America and all over the world that says God wants His people to be poor.

As a result, many people's minds have been so cluttered with garbage that they can't even think straight. They think, *Well,*

I'm having a financial difficulty. God must be trying to teach me something.

They read Psalm 35:27 this way: "Let them shout for joy, and be glad, that favor my righteous cause: yea, let them say continually, God wants me broke."

That's not what this verse of Scripture says. It says: *"...let them say continually, Let the Lord be magnified, which hath pleasure in the prosperity of his servant."*

God wants to see His people prosper. Under the Old Covenant, the Israelites were servants of God who brought pleasure to the heart of God through their prosperity. How much more today do we as believers, as sons and daughters of God, as children of the most high God, bring pleasure to the heart of God when we do well financially?

Bringing Pleasure to the Heart of God

Jesus asked, *"If ye then, being evil, know how to give good gifts unto your children, how much more shall your Father which is in heaven give good things to them that ask him?"* (Matthew 7:11).

Those of us who are parents are always trying to help our children and bless them. If we, falling so far below God's goodness, do this for our children, how much more does our Heavenly Father give good things to those who ask Him?

As children of God and joint heirs with Jesus Christ, we have been given the blessing of the Lord.

According to Proverbs 10:22, *"The blessing of the Lord...maketh rich, and he addeth no sorrow with it."* As believers, we become enriched in our souls when we know the Lord. The word *rich* here has only one meaning, and that is for financial prosperity. It is a word that describes wealth, money, income. We could quote Proverbs 10:22 this way: "The blessing of the Lord, it maketh financial prosperity." There is a prosperity that can come from the world. But the world's system is vicious, and the prosperity it offers brings sorrow with it. You are a child of God. Your Heavenly Father longs to pour out on you, as His child, blessings that bring no sorrow with them.

When you receive a bill in the mail, your first question should not be, "How am I going to pay it?" Your first question should be, "I wonder how my Heavenly Father is going to bring it to me this time?"

You Have to Know What's Yours

Sometimes I am asked, "If it's God's will for every believer to prosper, then why are so many dear Christian brothers and sisters still experiencing poverty and lack?" Because their souls have not been trained in this truth. Their understanding of the Scriptures has not been renewed to include all the promises of God.

In 3 John 2, God's Word clearly promises financial prosperity as a blessing from God for every believer: *"Beloved, I wish [or will] above all things that thou mayest prosper and be in health...."* Notice what the rest of that verse says: *"even as thy soul prospereth."*

You will prosper in proportion to the prosperity of your soul—and that comes in accordance with your understanding of the Word and your obedience to that Word. God's Word says, *"And this is the confidence that we have in him, that, if we ask any thing according to his will, he heareth us: And if we know that he hear us, whatsoever we ask, we know that we have the petitions that we desired of him"* (1 John 5:14-15).

Knowledge of the will of God is essential for you to have faith in your prayers. I remember some wonderful words shared by Kenneth E. Hagin in a meeting several years ago. They were so powerfully true I can't improve upon them. He said, "Faith can never rise above the known will of God."

You can't believe for something when you don't know if it's God's will for you to receive it. It's not just having a covenant with God; it's being a doer of the Word that releases these blessings. But if you don't know the Word, how can you be a doer of the Word? You will only prosper in proportion to the prosperity of your soul, or your understanding of the Scriptures.

When you know it's God's will for you to be saved, you have faith to be saved. When you know it's God's will for you to be healed, you can feed your spirit with promises of divine healing from God's Word and have faith to be healed. Prosperity is just like any promise, any blessing or any other provision of your redemption in God through Christ Jesus.

Prosperity—God's Perfect Will

Let yourself see financial prosperity for what it scripturally and actually is—a part of your redemption, which Jesus Christ died and paid for. You have to see prosperity in that light.

Prosperity is not an option. It's not something God just tolerates or allows you to have in His permissive will. Prosperity is one of the things the precious blood of Jesus was shed to purchase for you. Renew your mind to this truth. Prosperity was

55

bought and paid for by Jesus Christ. It is the perfect will of God for your life.

As soon as you become convinced of that, divine prosperity will become more than a right. It will become a daily reality in your life.

That's when you will begin praying with the aggressiveness necessary to actually transfer wealth out of the kingdom of darkness and into the hands of God's people in these last days. That's what the devil is fighting.

God wants you to prosper. He absolutely takes pleasure in you *"always having all sufficiency in all things"* so that you *"may abound to every good work"* (2 Corinthians 9:8).

Are you willing to please God by being prosperous?

10% of Your Income... 100% of Your Heart

Chapter 5

Gloria Copeland

"Bring ye all the tithes into the storehouse, that there may be meat in mine house, and prove me now herewith, saith the LORD of hosts, if I will not open you the windows of heaven, and pour you out a blessing, that there shall not be room enough to receive it. And I will rebuke the devourer for your sakes, and he shall not destroy the fruits of your ground; neither shall your vine cast her fruit before the time in the field, saith the LORD of hosts. And all nations shall call you blessed: for ye shall be a delightsome land, saith the LORD of hosts."
— MALACHI 3:10-12

Are you ready to take the limits off your income? I am! And the Lord has been showing me how we can do it.

I'm excited about it because this is the day when we as believers need to prosper.

We need to have enough not just to meet our own needs, but to see to it that the gospel is preached around the world.

Jesus is coming back soon! We don't have time to sit around wishing we had enough money to go through the doors God is opening before us. We don't have time to say, "Well, one day when finances aren't so tight, I'll give to this ministry or that one so they can buy television time in Eastern Europe, or print books in Spanish." We need to increase so we can give—and we need to do it now!

How do we get on that road to increase? I can tell you in two simple words: through tithing. In the plan of God, tithing and wealth are so closely connected that in the Hebrew language, they both come from the same root word.

Tithing is the covenant transaction that opens the door for God to be directly involved in our increase. It is a two-way exchange in which we honor God by giving Him 10 percent of our income and He, in return, provides us with a *"surplus of prosperity"* (Deuteronomy 28:11, *The Amplified Bible*).

You can see how that transaction works in Malachi 3:10-12. There the Lord says:

> Bring all the tithes—the whole tenth of your income—into the storehouse, that there may be food in My house, and prove Me now by it, says the Lord of hosts, if I will not open the windows of Heaven for you and pour you out a blessing, that there shall not be room enough to receive it. And I will rebuke the devourer...for your sakes, and he shall not destroy the fruits of your ground; neither shall your vine drop its fruit before the time in the field, says the Lord of hosts. And all nations shall call you happy and blessed; for you shall be a land of delight, says the Lord of hosts (*The Amplified Bible*).

More Than a Religious Routine

"But Gloria," you may say, "I know Christians who have been tithing for years and they're not wealthy!"

Actually, you don't. You just know people who have put 10 percent of their income into the offering bucket. They went through the motions, but they weren't really tithing. We've all done that at times.

You see, tithing isn't just a matter of the pocketbook. It is a matter of the heart. That's the way it is with everything as far as God is concerned. He always looks on the heart. So when we tithe as a religious routine, not in faith, just because we're supposed to and not as a genuine expression of our love for God, we miss out on the blessings of it.

That's what happened to the people in Malachi's day. They were bringing sacrifices to the Lord. They were going through the motions of tithing. But they were not being blessed. In fact, they were living under a financial curse because the attitude of their heart was not right.

In Malachi 1, we can read what the Lord had to say to them:

A son honors his father, and a servant his master. If then I am a

father, where is My honor? And if I am a master, where is the [reverent] fear due Me? says the Lord of hosts to you, O priests, who despise My name. You say, How and in what have we despised Your name? By offering polluted food upon My altar. And you ask, How have we polluted it and profaned You? ...When you priests offer blind [animals] for sacrifice, is it no evil? And when you offer the lame and the sick, is it no evil? Present such a thing...now to your governor [in payment of your taxes, and see what will happen]. Will he be pleased with you? Or will he receive you graciously? says the Lord of hosts (verses 6-8, *The Amplified Bible*).

What was missing from the tithes and offerings of these people? Honor! They weren't giving God their best. Because they didn't love and reverence God in their hearts, they were offering Him their leftovers. They were fulfilling religious requirements by keeping a formula with no worship.

As tithers, we should learn a lesson from them. When we find ourselves suffering financial lack and failing to enjoy the supernatural increase God has promised, we should check our attitude—fast! We should make sure we're giving God our best (not our leftovers) and honoring Him with all our heart.

Stick With God's Plan

If you're not sure whether your heart is right, here is one good way to tell. Check your attitude at offering time. Malachi 1:13 tells us what the Israelites' attitude was. They said, *"Behold, what a drudgery and weariness this is!"*

Have you ever had that thought when you were writing out your tithe check? Have you ever wanted to hide your pocketbook from God so you wouldn't have to give? If so, you need to change your attitude or it will prevent you from receiving your financial harvest. It will stop your increase.

Refuse to harbor such dishonorable thoughts toward God in your heart. Rebuke them and say, "No! I will not have that attitude. I love God and I love to give my tithe!"

Actually, we ought to be like little children when it comes to giving. Have you ever noticed how excited children get when their parents give them some money to put in the offering? They can hardly wait to give it.

We ought to be the same way. We ought to look forward to giving our tithes and offerings all week long.

"Well, it's hard to have that attitude now," you might say. "After all, I'm not a child anymore. No one is giving me any money."

God is! He is the One Who gives you everything you have. He owns everything on this earth because He made it. He will give you possessions if you will honor Him in joy with the firstfruits of your increase.

Of course, some people try to come up with their own plan. They'll say, "I can't really afford to give a full 10 percent, so I'll just give five." But that won't work because the Bible says the first tenth already belongs to the Lord. If we give Him anything less, we're robbing Him (Malachi 3:8). Leviticus 27 says it this way: *"...no thing that a man shall devote to the Lord of all that he has, whether of man or beast or of the field of his possession, shall be sold or redeemed; every devoted thing is most holy to the Lord...And all the tithe of the land, whether of the seed of the land or of the fruit of the tree, is the Lord's; it is holy to the Lord"* (verses 28, 30, *The Amplified Bible*).

Just as tithing opens the door to increase and the blessings of God, stealing God's tithe and using it on yourself opens the door to decrease and the financial destruction the devil brings. You'll never come out ahead by keeping the tithe.

Ken and I know that from personal experience. Right after we were born again, before we had much revelation of the Word, we'd try tithing for a few months. Then we'd decide we needed the money more than God did, so we'd stop. As a result, we just kept on decreasing financially. We kept on getting deeper in debt.

When we began to learn and obey God's Word, we made up our minds to tithe first, no matter what. That's when our finances turned around. We began to increase and we've been increasing ever since, praise God! Today if I had to choose between paying my tithe or having food to eat—I'd skip the food and pay my tithe because I know the blessings tithing in faith will bring.

Don't Forget Faith

When you really understand what a great deal tithing is, you'll have a hard time not getting excited about it! You'll want to jump and shout and praise God every time you think about it. You won't begrudge God His 10 percent, you'll thank Him for letting it flow through your hands.

He didn't have to do that, you know. He could have just given us the 90 percent and withheld the 10. He could withhold 90 and give us 10! But He didn't. He gave it to us so we could use it to keep the door of prosperity open. He gave it to us so we could return it and establish a covenant of blessing with Him.

Do you realize what a wonderful privilege it is to have a financial covenant with Almighty God? Do you understand what it means to be connected to His heavenly economy?

It means we don't have to worry about depression or recession—there is no recession or depression in heaven. It means we can sleep peacefully at night when the rest of the world is tormented by fear of financial failure. It means when the devil comes to steal our increase we can stand firmly on that covenant and say, "Get out of here, Satan! You're rebuked! We're tithers and the Word of God says you cannot devour our money. You can't devour our children. You can't devour our health. We've given God the firstfruits of all our increase so we are blessed. And what God has blessed, you can't curse!"

Oddly enough, there are some Christians who shrink back at such bold words. "Well, I just don't know if I could say that," they protest. "I'm a tither, but I'm still not as rich as the sinner down the street. So I'm not sure tithing does that much good."

The people in Malachi's day said exactly the same thing. They said, *"...It is useless to serve God; and what profit is it if we keep His ordinances?...And now we consider the proud and arrogant happy and favored; evildoers are exalted and prosper..."* (Malachi 3:14-15, *The Amplified Bible*).

God didn't like those words. He said they were hard and stout against Him. Why? Because they were words of unbelief instead of words of faith.

You see, God not only wants us to tithe in honor and love, He also wants us to tithe in faith! It takes faith to please Him (Hebrews 11:6).

If you don't have faith that God will prosper you, then get your Bible and study the promises He has made to you as a tither. For *"faith cometh by hearing, and hearing by the word of God"* (Romans 10:17). Meditate the Word so you can tithe believing that God will keep His end of the covenant and bless you abundantly.

God loves it when you tithe with that kind of confidence. He enjoys it when you give with an attitude of reverence and grati-tude, trusting Him to take care of you.

In fact, Malachi 3:16-17 says:

Then those who feared the Lord talked often one to another; and the Lord listened and heard it, and a book of remembrance was written before Him of those who reverenced and worshipfully feared the Lord, and who thought on His name. And they shall be Mine, says the Lord of hosts, in that day when I publicly recognize and openly declare them to be My jewels—My special possession, My peculiar treasure. And I will spare them, as a man spares his own son who serves him *(The Amplified Bible).*

Don't you want to be counted as one of God's special treasures? I certainly do! First of all, because I love God and I want to be pleasing to Him. Second, because I know how I treat special treasures. I keep my eye on them. I take good care of them, and if I'm God's special treasure, that's exactly how He'll treat me!

"Lord...Bless Me!"

The fact is, God has already treated us with overwhelming kindness. He has already given us all more than we ever dreamed possible. He has saved us. He has provided healing for us. He has blessed us in a thousand different ways. And that's what we should remember every time we tithe. We should come before the Lord and thank Him for bringing us into our promised land. Tithe with an attitude of gratitude.

If you'll read Deuteronomy 26, you'll see that's what He instructed the Israelites to do. He didn't want them to simply plunk their tithe without putting their heart into it. He commanded them to come very purposefully and worship Him with it, saying:

> ...A wandering and lost Aramean ready to perish was my father [Jacob], and he went down into Egypt, and sojourned there, few in number, and he became there a nation, great, mighty, and numerous. And the Egyptians treated us very badly, and afflicted us, and

69

laid upon us hard bondage. And when we cried to the Lord, the God of our fathers, the Lord heard our voice, and looked on our affliction, and our labor, and our (cruel) oppression; And the Lord brought us forth out of Egypt with a mighty hand, and with an outstretched arm, and with great (awesome) power, and with signs, and with wonders; And He brought us into this place, and gave us this land, a land flowing with milk and honey. And now, behold, I bring the first fruits of the ground, which You, O Lord, have given me (verses 5-10, *The Amplified Bible*).

We would do well to say much the same thing each time we tithe. To say, "Father, once I was lost, a prisoner of sin with no hope and no covenant with You. But You sent Jesus to redeem me. You sent Him to shed His precious blood so I could be free. Thank You, Lord, for delivering me out of the kingdom of darkness and translating me into the kingdom of Your dear

Son. Thank You for receiving my tithe as an expression of worship to You."

But we shouldn't stop with that. We should also say as the Israelites did, "Now, Lord, I have brought the tithe out of my house. I haven't kept it for myself. But I've given it just as You have commanded. So look down from Your holy habitation, from heaven, and bless me!" (see verses 13-15).

Does that kind of talk make you nervous? Do you think God will be offended if you tell Him to bless you? He won't! He'll be delighted. After all, blessing us was His idea. It's what He has wanted to do all along.

So don't be shy. Tithe boldly! Tithe gladly! Give God 10 percent of your income and 100 percent of your heart. Then rejoice in faith and say continually, "Let the Lord be magnified, Who takes pleasure in the prosperity of His servant!"

Begin to expect!

Take the limits off God and let Him have a good time prospering you!

The Tithe—
Is It for Today?

Chapter 6

"Bring ye all the tithes into the storehouse, that there may be meat in mine house, and prove me now herewith, saith the LORD of hosts, if I will not open you the windows of heaven, and pour you out a blessing, that there shall not be room enough to receive it."

— MALACHI 3:10

Kenneth Copeland

It amazes me how many believers waste their energies arguing whether or not tithing is a New Testament doctrine. I've heard people say, "Tithing is under the law! We're not under the law, we're under grace. That's why I don't tithe. Oh, I give offerings, but I don't tithe." People who think this way are self-deceived.

Tithing didn't begin with the law! According to Genesis 4:1-4, before the law was ever given to Moses, Abel and Cain brought the firstfruits of their labor to God.

And again in Genesis 14, we find that Abraham tithed—**before the law!** Abraham and 318 of his armed servants had conquered a group of enemy kings, slaughtered them, and took the spoils. And the very first thing Abram did was tithe the spoils. Melchizedek, the priest, blessed Abram and said, *"Blessed be Abram of the most high God, possessor of heaven and earth: And blessed be the most high God, which hath delivered thine enemies into thy hand. And he gave him tithes of all"* (verses 19-20). So tithing didn't begin with the law. The law only explained the tithe, gave it procedure, and demanded it.

But, is tithing under the New Covenant as well? To answer this question, let's first read Hebrews 7:1-8.

For this Melchisedec, king of Salem, priest of the most high God, who met Abraham returning from the slaughter of the kings, and blessed him; To whom also Abraham gave a tenth part of all; first being by interpretation King of righteousness, and after that also King

of Salem, which is, King of peace; Without father, without mother, without descent, having neither beginning of days, nor end of life; but made like unto the Son of God; abideth a priest continually. Now consider how great this man was, unto whom even the patriarch Abraham gave the tenth of the spoils. And verily they that are of the sons of Levi, who receive the office of the priesthood, have a commandment to take tithes of the people according to the law, that is, of their brethren, though they come out of the loins of Abraham: But he whose descent is not counted from them received tithes of Abraham, and blessed him that had the promises. And without all contradiction the less is blessed of the better. And here men that die receive tithes; but there he receiveth them, of whom it is witnessed that he liveth.

What do these verses mean? Simply this, that Melchizedek was a man whose birth was not on record. His genealogy could not be traced back to Levi (or the tribe of the priesthood). Nevertheless Melchizedek was made a priest by God and received Abraham's tithes. You cannot argue that tithing is just under the law because this happened four hundred years before the law.

Hebrews 5:6 tells us that Jesus is a High Priest after the order of Melchizedek. He has all the rights that Melchizedek had, which included the right to bless the tithe. Under the New Covenant, Jesus not only receives our tithes, He blesses them and then blesses us just as Abraham was blessed. Why? Because as Galatians 3:14 says, *"...the blessing of Abraham [has] come on the Gentiles through Jesus Christ"*! The day that Melchizedek blessed Abraham, that very blessing was handed to you and me through Jesus Christ—our High Priest after the order of Melchizedek! If Melchizedek blessed Abraham, then how much more will Jesus bless us!

How do we activate that blessing? By placing our faith in the Word of God, and faith without actions of obedience to back it up is dead (James 2:17, *The Amplified Bible*). Since true faith is acting on what you believe, if you believe that you are blessed with faithful Abraham, you will do what he did—tithe to your Faithful High Priest!

Tithing activates the blessing of God in your finances. Read Malachi 3:10-12. There God promises that when you tithe, He'll rebuke the devil and command him to keep his hands off your finances. And that promise is as good today as it ever was because when God rebukes the devil, he stays rebuked!

So if you want to involve Almighty God in your finances,

> **Bring ye all the tithes into the storehouse, that there may be meat in mine house, and prove me now herewith, saith the LORD of hosts, if I will not open you the windows of heaven, and pour you out a blessing, that there shall not be room enough to receive it. And I will rebuke the devourer for your sakes, and he shall**

not destroy the fruits of your ground; neither shall your vine cast her fruit before the time in the field, saith the LORD of hosts. And all nations shall call you blessed: for ye shall be a delightsome land, saith the LORD of hosts.

Yes! Tithing is part of the New Covenant. Don't wait until your back is against the wall before you use your faith in the financial realm. Begin tithing while things are going well. Learn to act on the Word now, and when Satan tries to pin you against the wall, you can smile and know that you have it made. His power over you financially has been stopped! When you stand on the covenant of God and exercise your rights as a tither, Satan has no chance against you.

The Power to Prosper

"Christ hath redeemed us from the curse of the law, being made a curse for us: for it is written, Cursed is every one that hangeth on a tree: That the blessing of Abraham might come on the Gentiles through Jesus Christ; that we might receive the promise of the Spirit through faith."
— GALATIANS 3:13-14

Kenneth Copeland

A little sickness here...a pinch in the finances there...that's how the devil tries to bully you out of your blessings. Don't let him do it! Stand firm in the faith and kick a little sand in his face for a change. After all, you're no weakling. You've been given—the power to prosper.

"You were blessed."

"You are blessed."

"You will be blessed."

Do you recognize what these sentences represent? They are the past, present and future tenses of the verb "to bless."

Don't worry, I'm not going to give you a grammar lesson. I'm going to give you a lesson in living! You see, if you're going to enjoy the full and prosperous life God has made available to you, you're going to have to realize that His blessings cover the past, present and future! The following story from Luke 13 perfectly illustrates this point.

And he [Jesus] was teaching in one of the synagogues on the sabbath. And, behold, there was a woman which had a spirit of infirmity eighteen years, and was bowed together, and could in no wise lift up herself. And when Jesus saw her, he called her to him, and said unto her, Woman, thou art loosed from thine infirmity. And he laid his hands on her: and immediately she was made straight, and glorified God. And the ruler of the synagogue answered with indignation, because that Jesus had healed on the sabbath day, and said unto the people, There are six days in which men ought to work: in them therefore come and be

healed, and not on the sabbath day. The Lord then answered him, and said, Thou hypocrite, doth not each one of you on the sabbath loose his ox or his ass from the stall, and lead him away to watering? And ought not this woman, being a daughter of Abraham, whom Satan hath bound, lo, these eighteen years, be loosed from this bond on the sabbath day? (verses 10-16).

First of all, I want you to notice that Jesus called this little lady a daughter of Abraham. By using this terminology, He was pointing out that she had a very special relationship with Almighty God. She had a covenant relationship with Him, a bond, a pact, and because of this, she could be set free from her infirmity.

I want you to also notice that Jesus didn't tell her that maybe some day she might be loosed from her infirmity. No, He said, "You are loosed," present tense. Jesus knew that she was a covenant woman. In His mind, her healing was already provided.

God is always operating in the present tense. He never forgets what He has provided for His children. His covenant is ever close to His heart.

In order to receive from God, you must realize that His Word is His bond, and regardless of how much time passes, the depth of His commitment never wanes. It remains fresh in the mind of God regardless of whether His people remember it or not.

That is why Jesus could tell that little woman, "You are loosed from this infirmity." Because God was still mindful of His Word to Abraham. And the day He spoke to Abram, 700 years before she was born, that little lady was in Abraham's loins. If the promises were made for anyone, they were made for her!

In fact, the covenant was made to everyone in that synagogue. They just didn't know it. They were so mindful of their traditions they didn't even know what the Master was talking about. They became angry with Him for healing on the Sabbath!

As a Christian, you have a covenant with Almighty God. It is just as binding as the one Abraham had, only it is a better covenant with better promises (Hebrews 8:6). To get an understanding of your covenant provisions, let's look at Galatians 3:6-14:

> Even as Abraham believed God, and it was accounted to him for righteousness. Know ye therefore that they which are of faith, the same are the children of Abraham. And the scripture, foreseeing that God would justify the heathen through faith, preached before the gospel unto Abraham, saying, In thee shall all nations be blessed. So then they which be of faith are blessed with faithful Abraham. For as many as are of the works of the law are under the curse: for it is written, Cursed is every one that continueth not in all things which are written in the book of the law to do them.
>
> But that no man is justified by the law in the sight of God, it is

evident: for, The just shall live by faith. And the law is not of faith: but, The man that doeth them shall live in them. Christ hath redeemed us from the curse of the law, being made a curse for us: for it is written, Cursed is every one that hangeth on a tree: That the blessing of Abraham might come on the Gentiles through Jesus Christ; that we might receive the promise of the Spirit through faith.

I want you to notice how many times the word "bless" is used in this passage of scripture. Unfortunately, this word is too often heard as merely a religious term, and very few people understand the real meaning of it. But God is very exact in His usage of this word; He doesn't take it lightly.

The phrase "to bless" is used mainly in a covenant relationship. You begin to understand its meaning when you study the covenant that God has entered with us. When He joined Himself irrevocably to us, we had nothing to give Him. We were totally spiritually bankrupt with nothing to offer Him while He, on the other hand, is

Almighty God, all-powerful and the possessor of heaven and earth. He took our spiritual bankruptcy and exchanged it for His life and nature. He took our sinfulness and exchanged it for His righteousness. He took our sicknesses and carried our diseases and gave us divine healing. Hallelujah!

And you'll notice that in verses 13-14, He took the curse for us so that we might be blessed with faithful Abraham through Jesus Christ. What does that mean? The best way I know to describe the term *to bless* is to "empower one to prosper." To *prosper* means "to excel in something that is desirable as well as good."

To be spiritually blessed would be to be empowered to prosper spiritually. To prosper spiritually would first of all mean being born again. You could not excel spiritually if you still had the sin nature. But on the other hand, once you are born again, you can excel to the point of being baptized in the Holy Ghost, hearing the voice of the Lord, exhibiting the nature and character of God in your daily life, and operating in the gifts of the Spirit. To be spiritually blessed according to the Bible means to be empowered to excel in that which is desirable to the Holy Spirit. If you are spiritually blessed, there is no limit to how much you can prosper in the spirit realm.

To be blessed physically means to be empowered to prosper in your physical body, to be healthy and vibrant and able to accomplish the will of God for your life. It is not God's will for the devil to hinder you and keep you bound by sickness and disease.

To be blessed mentally means to be empowered to prosper in your mind. It includes being emotionally sound. It also means being able to understand the Word and spiritual things. It means having your mind renewed with God's Word.

Now, what do you think it means to be cursed? That is also a covenant term, and its true meaning is "to empower to fail."

Let's read Galatians 3:13-14 again in this new light. Using our definitions, let's see how the meaning of these verses expands our understanding of our covenant with God. "Christ has redeemed us from being empowered to fail by being empowered to fail for us: for it is written, Empowered to fail is every one who hangs on a tree: That the empowerment to prosper from Abraham might come on the Gentiles through Jesus Christ; that we might receive the promise of the Spirit through faith." (You can go to Deuteronomy 28:1-13 and find out exactly what the blessings of Abraham are. Rather than reading them the way they are written in the *King James Version,* read them with the Bible definition of the word "bless.")

With this in mind, consider the following statement God made to Abraham. *"And I will bless them that bless thee, and curse him that curseth thee: and in thee shall all families of the earth be blessed"* (Genesis 12:3). Again, using our definition, let's read it this way, "I will empower those to prosper who empower you to prosper. And I will empower those to fail who try to cause you to fail."

In other words, "Anyone who has your best interest at heart, I will empower to prosper. And anyone who does not have your best interest at heart, I will cause their efforts to fail." If you are in covenant with God, you are destined to succeed! Anyone who comes against your success is coming against your covenant. God will stop their efforts to hurt you, not because He doesn't love them, not because He prefers you, but because He is bound by His Word. God loves everyone equally and wants everyone to be blessed.

So what will keep you in a state of always being empowered by God to prosper? Seek to empower those around you to prosper in every area of their lives—spiritually, mentally, physically, financially and socially. If you bless others, God will bless you!

Galatians 3:29 promises that the blessings of Abraham are yours in Christ. *"And if ye be Christ's, then are ye Abraham's seed, and heirs according to the promise."* Notice again that this is in the present tense. If you are in Christ, you are Abraham's seed and an heir according to the promise made to Abraham.

Just like the little lady in Luke, you are loosed from your infirmity. You are empowered to prosper in every area of your life—right now! Don't put it off to the future—some day in the sweet by-and-by—or think that it passed away with the first disciples. You are empowered to prosper today!

Better Than Miracles

Chapter 8

"The LORD shall increase you more and more, you and your children."
— PSALM 115:14

Jerry Savelle

How many Christians do you know right now who are just barely hanging on financially? How many do you know who are looking for a miracle to get them through a critical time of shortage and lack? Unless I miss my guess, you know quite a few. You may even be among them yourself.

If so, I know what you're going through. Financially speaking, several years ago, I went through the toughest years of my life and ministry. During that time it seemed the pressure never ceased. It's not that God didn't deliver us. He did! He rescued us from disaster over and over again.

Yet as soon as one financial miracle came—another impossible situation rose up right behind it. We literally lived from one financial miracle to the next.

I don't mind telling you that, even though I was grateful for those miracles (and this ministry wouldn't have survived without them), I got tired of living that way.

"Well, Brother Jerry, isn't that just part of living by faith?" you ask. "Isn't it God's plan for us to believe Him every day for enough to get by?"

No, it isn't.

God has impressed on me that His will for us is much higher than that.

A Covenant of Increase

You see, God's covenant with us isn't a "just get by" covenant. It's a covenant of supernatural increase. That's proven again and again throughout the Bible. Psalm 115 says:

O Israel, trust thou in the LORD: he is their help and their shield. O house of Aaron, trust in the LORD: he is their help and their shield. Ye that fear the LORD, trust in the LORD: he is their help and their shield. The LORD hath been mindful of us: he will bless us; he will bless the house of Israel; he will bless the house of Aaron. He will bless them that fear the LORD, both small and great. The LORD shall increase you more and more, you and your children (verses 9-14).

God has made a solemn, covenant vow to increase you. How much will He increase you? More and more! In other words, His increase is unlimited. That means no matter how much increase you have experienced up to now, you still haven't seen all the increase God has in store for you.

I know material wealth makes religious people nervous, but God has no problem with it. It wouldn't bother Him at all if it took every bank in town to hold all your increase, as long as you remembered and honored Him as the God of increase. (See Deuteronomy 8:11.) In fact, Psalm 35:27 says the Lord *"hath pleasure in the prosperity of his servant"!*

No Interruptions, Please

God's kind of prosperity isn't sporadic, either. It doesn't just come occasionally to get you out of a financial jam. No, we've already seen that it increases you *"more and more."* The *R.K. Harrison Translation of Hebrew Into Current English* says it like this: *"May the Lord give you continual prosperity."*

Continual prosperity! Continual means without interruption. If there's no interruption in my prosperity, I won't have to live on financial miracles!

God gives us a picture of that kind of prosperity in Deuteronomy 8:6-9. There, He tells the Israelites:

> Therefore thou shalt keep the commandments of the LORD thy God, to walk in his ways, and to fear him. For the LORD thy God bringeth thee into a good land, a land of brooks of water, of fountains and depths that spring out of valleys and hills; A land of wheat, and barley, and vines, and fig trees, and pomegranates; a land of oil olive, and

**honey; A land wherein thou shalt eat
bread without scarceness, thou shalt
not lack any thing in it.**

Continual prosperity is a lifestyle without
scarceness. A lifestyle without lack. What's
more, Deuteronomy 28:11 says, *"The Lord
shall make you have a surplus of prosperity..." (The Amplified Bible).* A surplus
means there's more than enough!

Most of us have thought, if we could
just get our needs met, we'd be prosperous. But that's a shallow version of what
God calls prosperity. He says prosperity is
having a surplus. He says, *"A good man
leaveth an inheritance to his children's
children"* (Proverbs 13:22).

Notice how much higher His thoughts
are than our thoughts. In His estimation of
increase, not only are all your needs met,
but also you have enough left over to help
somebody else and enough in store for two
generations after you!

How do we walk in that kind of increase?
The first step is to begin to expect it. We'll
never experience continual, supernatural

prosperity until we elevate our thinking to God's level and enlarge our capacity to receive.

We must be able to see it happen with the eyes of our heart. When we have that image on the inside of us, God will be able to deliver it to us. Our only limitation is our own thinking.

A Reward for the Diligent

Let me warn you, though, this kind of increase is not something you're going to experience overnight. It's not something that will happen after just a week or two. It takes commitment.

God told Moses in Deuteronomy 28:1, *"...it shall come to pass, if thou shalt hearken diligently unto the voice of the LORD thy God, to observe and to do all his commandments...that the LORD thy God will set thee on high above all the nations of the earth."* *Diligence* means to make a steady effort to accomplish. A diligent person never backs off. Never quits. Never gives up.

As I've studied the Word, I've found that supernatural increase comes to faithful and diligent people. People who have a determination to hold fast to God's Word no matter how impossible the circumstances may seem.

Galatians 6:9 says, *"And let us not be weary in well doing: for in due season we shall reap, if we faint not."* There is a due season for those who are diligent and faithful. There is a set time, a designated moment when God rewards those who diligently seek Him (Hebrews 11:6).

Time for a Change

I want you to know, I've come to my "due season" and I'm enjoying it. I've enlarged my thinking and set my sights on the good land where there is no scarceness or lack. I intend to live in continual prosperity.

Since November 1992, when God began to deal with me about His covenant of supernatural increase, the financial blessings that have come in my ministry are as overwhelming and hard to keep up with as the pressure was previously. Our increase is so great, we can hardly contain it!

I've made up my mind, I'm not going to live from one financial miracle to the next anymore. If I can believe God to bail me out when I'm almost at rock bottom, then I can believe God for continual prosperity so I won't have to go through that kind of mess!

Praise God, I am blessed of the Lord, and as Proverbs 10:22 says, *"The blessing of the Lord, it maketh rich, and he addeth no sorrow with it."*

Now don't misunderstand. I'm not telling you to get your eyes on riches. I'm telling you to be faithful to God and simply expect Him to fulfill the covenant of increase.

If you'll do that, you won't have to get your eyes on riches and wealth. In fact, you won't even have to pursue them. They'll chase you down!

God said, *"...all these blessings shall come on thee, and overtake thee, if thou shalt hearken unto the voice of the Lord thy God"* (Deuteronomy 28:2). He didn't say you'd come on the blessings and overtake them.

If you're pursuing the blessings, you have it backward. Jesus said, *"...seek ye first the kingdom of God, and his right-eousness; and all these things shall be added unto you"* (Matthew 6:33).

Please note, however, that He did say, *"all these things shall be added."* I believe it's time for that "addition" to come. It's time for supernatural increase in the Body of Christ. We've been financially over-whelmed in the past—not only individually, but collectively. But that's about to change.

Due season has come. It's time for us to tear down the fences of limitation in our lives and believe God to enlarge our borders. It's time to stop living from financial miracle to financial miracle and start living in continual prosperity.

I'm ready, aren't you?

Name Your Seed!
Sow It...Don't Throw It!

Chapter 9

"Be not deceived; God is not mocked: for whatsoever a man soweth, that shall he also reap."
— GALATIANS 6:7

Jesse Duplantis

I'm going to catch me a thief!

Satan stole my harvest for years, but I found out why and I know how to stop him.

Let me explain. One of the very first things I began to do as a new believer was to give. I wasn't giving to get. I was giving because I wanted to do the kinds of things God did. Giving was the first thing I noticed about God. It's His nature to give. I picked that up immediately: *"For God so loved the world, that He gave"* (John 3:16).

From my first day as a new Christian, I was doing a good job of fulfilling the first part of Malachi 3:10: *"Bring ye all the tithes into the storehouse, that there may be meat in mine house...."* There was meat in my house and I was blessed as a giver. But then I discovered God wanted even more for me. I began to get excited every time I heard the second part of that verse: *"and prove me now herewith, saith the LORD of hosts, if I will not open you the windows of heaven, and pour you out a blessing, that there shall not be room enough to receive it."*

But despite the fact that I was a faithful giver, I could not say I had been blessed to the point that I didn't have room for more. Why?

One day when I was jogging, the Lord began to deal with me about that.

You know, what you sow is what you reap, He said. *You know you've always had everything met—your needs have always been met.*

"That's right," I said.

But are you at the point in your life where you cannot receive any more blessing?

"No," I answered.

Let Me tell you something, Jesse. For years you never named your seed.

He was right. I didn't know how many times I had given gifts—sometimes quite large gifts for me—in obedience to the Lord. Then months later, I would be walking past great fields of harvest that I didn't know were mine. I would see harvests everywhere and think, *God, this is what I need for my ministry.*

Because I didn't know what kind of seed I had sown, I didn't know what kind of harvest to expect. I didn't know I was walking past my harvests. As a result, the devil was able to control what belonged to me. He was standing by those harvests with his guards saying, "That's not yours. This is the wealth of the wicked. You are the just."

Satan was able to do it because I never named my seed. I didn't know what I put in the ground, so how was I to know when it came back thirty-, sixty-, a hundredfold?

Sown or Thrown?

I was not operating according to a basic principle—sowing and reaping. Galatians 6:7 says, *"Be not deceived; God is not mocked:*

*for whatsoever a man soweth, that shall he
also reap."*

"Whatsoever" you put in the ground is
going to come up. "Whatsoever" encom-
passes all human activity. All our acts are
forces. Every time we think, every time we
feel, every time we exercise our will, we are
sowing. So we have to consider our ways
and give thought to what we are sowing. If
you consider what you are sowing, then
you will recognize your harvest.

What you sow is what you reap is the
law of Genesis 1:12, that every seed repro-
duces after its kind: *"And the earth brought
forth grass, and herb yielding seed after his
kind, and the tree yielding fruit, whose seed
was in itself, after his kind: and God saw
that it was good."*

All of life, everything you do, is a process
of sowing. You sow clothes, you get clothes.
You sow healing, you get healing.

I told a lady one time, "I want to pray
for you so I can feel better."

"No, you mean so I can feel better."

"No, so I can feel better," I said. After I prayed for her, I said, "Oh, I feel better."

"So do I," she said.

"Go sow. Go sow," I said. "More health will come to you."

Understand what tithing does. It meets the general operating expense of the church, such as salaries, light bills and upkeep. When you brought meat to God's house, that meat met the necessities of God's house. Because you met the necessities of God's house, you harvested provision to meet the necessities of your house.

But when you gave an offering above the tithe without naming it, you were throwing it instead of sowing it, and you lost it before you got out the door. You would see a need and throw money at it, not even thinking about naming the type of seed you were sowing or naming your harvest. That seed would land on top of the ground and before you got out the church door, the devil would steal it.

So, you were eating and paying the light bill, but you continued to face the loan payments.

That's not what God wants. He wants His people to be blessed. He wants His Church to be out of debt. The Church will be out of debt when the people are out of debt. Deception has kept God's people without their full entitlement.

Sow Specific Seed

I don't care if it's 2 cents, name your seed. When you give your child $3, $2, a quarter and you say, "Put this in the Sunday school offering," ask him what he's believing for.

Out West not long ago I had a little 7-year-old boy walk up to me wearing a big, silver belt buckle, starched and creased jeans and a western shirt. With tears in his eyes he said, "I want to give to your television ministry."

He gave me $7. Now that's a lot of money for a 7-year-old. I almost went, "No, little fellow." But the Lord said, *What are you doing? Ask him what he's believing for.*

So I told him, "You have given me a seed. If you don't name this seed you're going to lose this money. And seven bucks is a lot of money to lose."

"That's right," he said.

"What are you believing for?" I asked. "Name your seed, little fellow."

"A four-wheeler wouldn't be bad."

"Anything else? This is a big seed."

"And a horse."

I said, "Fine. Now this is a horse and a four-wheeler. Isn't that wonderful? The devil can't rob you, son. You have planted your seed. You're motivated by love. You've named it. You're not deceived. You're not mocking God. You've got it coming."

"Thank you," he said. Then he asked me if he could hug me. He hugged my leg and off he went.

That was in the basement of the church. Right after that I met the boy's father in the foyer of the church and he told me how proud he was of his son, how his son was a hard worker and had never asked for a dime.

"It's kind of strange," he said. "I don't know if I know the voice of God as much as some of you ministers, but let me just ask you a question. This morning I was driving to church and the Lord...I don't know if it was the Lord or not...my wife and I were talking, and we thought about maybe buying the kid a four-wheeler...."

"Has your son ever asked you for a four-wheeler?" I asked.

"He never asks me for anything. He's a hard little worker...He delivers papers. He does all kinds of things. And my wife said, 'Let's get him a horse, too.'"

"When are you planning on doing that?" I asked.

"I'm thinking about doing it this afternoon."

I told him, "You know, you ought to obey God."

Now, if I had said to that little boy, "Thank you, brother, for blessing the ministry. Come here, little fellow, let me bless you," that would have been a thoughtless gesture on my part. That little boy would not have named his seed, and you will never make me believe, if he hadn't named his seed, he would have gotten his horse or his four-wheeler.

Leaving a Money Trail

Thoughtlessness is the beginning of great loss. Thoughtlessness can result in giving that is not properly motivated. It can also result in failure to name your seed.

Haggai 1:4-6 warns believers to be thoughtful givers: *"Is it time for you, O ye, to dwell in your cieled houses, and this [God's] house lie waste? Now therefore thus saith the LORD of hosts; Consider your ways. Ye have sown much, and bring in little...he that earneth wages earneth wages to put it into a bag with holes."*

You may be a faithful giver and yet be a thoughtless giver. You pay off your monthly obligations but never have anything left over. How does the devil always know where you are? You're leaving a trail of money for him to follow.

Haggai says you have *"sown much, and bring in little"*...and the bag into which you put your wages has holes in it. Throwing seed on top of the ground is like putting money in a bag full of holes. Satan will walk right behind you picking up that thrown seed so he can invest it in his people.

Don't be a thoughtless giver. Purpose in your heart what you will give. Second Corinthians 9:7 says, *"Every man according as he purposeth in his heart, so let him give; not grudgingly, or of necessity: for God loveth a cheerful giver."* Regard your giving as an act of worship. Make sure you are motivated by love—by the desire to bless, rather than the desire to get. Then name your seed. If you do, you will be in line for a blessing.

You don't have to let the devil control what belongs to you. I asked the Lord one time about Proverbs 13:22: *"...the wealth of the sinner is laid up for the just."* That sounded like Robin Hood stuff to me. Why would He take from those people and give to me? Rob from the rich and give to the poor?

Jesse, your ancestors for centuries have been giving and throwing seed instead of sowing seed, He said. *The reason why the wealth of the wicked is laid up for the just is that's your ancestor's seed that they never named. That's My money, and if it's My money, it's your money because you're an heir with Me—a joint heir.*

That's why it's coming back. That's why He can go to get the wealth of the wicked and give it to you. God is very interested in your being out of debt. When He pulled the nation of Israel out of Egypt and set them free, He said, "Take My money. Get My money. Be not deceived." He's not letting the devil keep His money. Egypt owed Israel 400 years of labor. God said, "Get My money. Bring it out with you."

If you have named your seed, next time you pass your harvest, you can tell the devil, "Hey, that's my harvest. That's mine. Get off my property."

The Sector of Optimum Yield

Once you've named your seed, cultivate it. Think about it. You want it to come up. If you'll put fertilizer on it, keep the weeds away from it, and cultivate it, you'll get a higher yield—an optimum yield. Cultivation is the very act of thinking, *"Now faith is the substance of things hoped for, the evidence of things not seen"* (Hebrews 11:1).

I've given seed for my television ministry. I cultivate that seed. I tell Cathy, "Bless God, we gave this money over here, gave this money over there. That's coming in the Name of Jesus." I'm cultivating.

I'm not asking God to give me my money back. No. I want my harvest. It's going to happen, too. You can take it to the bank. The devil stole from me for too long. I tell you, I'm catching that thief and I'm getting back what's mine. I'm going back in my canceled check records and finding records of seed I planted and I'm naming it and calling it mine.

The Bible says if you catch the thief, he's got to return it sevenfold. I'm going to get too expensive for the devil to mess with.

I've only been to one Kenneth Hagin convention, but it was the most expensive pit stop I ever made in my life. The Lord told me what He wanted me to give, and I had trouble believing it. I leaned over to the guy next to me and asked, "Did you say anything?" Sweat was coming off his cheeks and he said the Lord had just told him to give that same amount. "I heard it, too," I said. "That must be yours. That's not mine."

But the Lord said, *I told you, too.*

"God."

What Jesse?

"That's all I got."

That's all I asked for.

I'll never forget that, but you know I lost my return on that seed. I don't mean it didn't get used for the Lord's work. I didn't get my return, because I never named it.

But you know what I did? I went back to those 1983 and '84 check records and found that Hagin seed. I went back in those bank records. I've gone to catch a thief. And every time I find a canceled check for a gift I've given, I say, "Aha, devil. You owe me seven times. You've got to pay me, boy!"

I'm not claiming it because it's money, praise God, but because it's my seed. It's my harvest.

I'm not looking for money.

Money's looking for me.

God says the wealth of the wicked is laid up for Jesse. When they come with my money, I'm going to say, "Bring it on in. Just bring it on in. Put it over here, bless God."

Miraculous Provision Is on the Way

Chapter 10

Mark Brazee

"...Go, borrow thee vessels abroad of all thy neighbours, even empty vessels; borrow not a few."
— 2 KINGS 4:3

One day while I was praying, asking the Lord about things to come—both in my ministry and in the Church overall—I heard one word in my spirit just as plain as could be.

Miracles.

I meditated on that for a while, thinking primarily about healing miracles—when the blind see, the deaf hear, the lame walk and the maimed are made whole. Then I decided to start studying what the Word has to say about miracles. What I discovered really jarred my thinking. And it gave me insight into not only *how,* but *why* God will cause miracles to be increasingly commonplace before Jesus returns.

Four Types of Miracles

Miracles—extraordinary events demonstrating divine intervention in human affairs—can be traced from Genesis to Revelation and divided into four main categories. There are physical miracles, such as the man at the gate called Beautiful, who went walking, leaping and praising God when Peter and John commanded him to be made whole. There are also provisional miracles, like when Jesus provided money for Peter to pay taxes. Peter found the money in the mouth of the fish.

Then, there are miracles of protection or deliverance—like when Peter was delivered out of prison by an angel, or when an angel appeared to Paul and told him all lives on board his sinking ship would be saved. Finally, there are signs and wonders that God performs—miracles that simply prove His power or existence—like when God caused the sun to move backward 10 degrees for Hezekiah.

Elijah, Elisha, Jesus

The first thing I noticed when I began to study miracles was that there were three main people in the Bible through whom God worked miracles: Elijah, Elisha and Jesus. They shared a striking similarity: They began and ended their ministries with provisional miracles.

Elijah's first miracle is recorded in 1 Kings 17, when he prayed and the rain stopped. Three years later, he prayed and it rained. That's provision. His last miracle occurred when he parted the Jordan River. He needed to get across and he didn't have a boat. He had to catch up with the chariot of fire that took him up to heaven. So Elijah parted the waters by striking them with his mantle, and provided himself access to the other side. That, too, was a provisional miracle.

Elisha began his ministry with a provisional miracle—the same kind that concluded Elijah's ministry. He needed to get across the river to enter into the fullness of his ministry, and it took divine intervention, in the ordinary course of nature, to transport him there.

He took the mantle that fell from Elijah, rolled it up, hit the waters of the Jordan River with it and said, *"Where now is the Lord, the God of Elijah?"*

117

(2 Kings 2:14, *New International Version*) and the river parted.

What about Elisha's last miracle? That, too, was provisional.

We find the account of it in 2 Kings 6. After the Syrians had surrounded Samaria and cut off all its supplies, the people of the city were starving to death. People were paying just about all the money they could get their hands on for an ass's head or a cab of dove's dung (2 Kings 6:25). They were even eating their own children. In the midst of this crisis, Elisha said by the Spirit of God, "Tomorrow at this time , you can find anything you want." In a miraculous act of provision, God used four lepers to plunder the enemy's camp and take everything they needed—silver, gold, food and clothing. This was Elisha's last miracle.

Jesus also began and ended His ministry on the earth with provisional miracles. At the wedding feast in Cana, He turned water into wine. Multiplying the loaves and the fish was a provisional miracle. Jesus' last miracle before His ascension took place after He arose from the dead. He was on the shore, watching Peter and some others fishing, when he called out to Peter, "Throw your net out the other side." When Peter did as he was told, his net caught 153 fish. Divine intervention prospered Peter's business tremendously, causing him to recognize the Lord immediately.

The Spirit of Elijah on the Church

When I began to study provisional miracles carefully, I discovered that God almost always performs provisional miracles first—before He performs the physical miracles. Now, that really jarred my thinking because I had always thought a physical miracle, such as healing, took priority over other miracles. But the Lord drew my attention to the beginning of all things—the book of Genesis.

The very first miracle recorded in Genesis is provisional. God created the world and everything in it *before* He created man. God didn't physically create man first and then temporarily suspend him in space while

He made provision for him. No. God made provision for man *first,* then He created him.

Once I caught the revelation of that order—first the provisional, then the physical miracle—I saw the significance of it throughout Scripture. Physical miracles always produce an increase. If no provision is made for that increase first, then the increase will be lost.

Do you see how that pertains to the harvest? In Acts 3:7, one man was healed. As a result, 5,000 people were added to the Church (Acts 4:4). Physical miracles produce increase. But what would happen if you had physical miracles without the proper provision to handle that increase?

As we come into the last days, the spirit of Elijah is going to fall upon the Church collectively, and not just on one individual singularly. The "spirit of Elijah" is the spirit of preparing for the coming of the Lord Jesus. As that anointing comes upon the Church we will experience the same flow of the miraculous that Elijah and Jesus experienced.

I find it interesting that when Elisha picked up Elijah's mantle, Elisha received a double portion of Elijah's anointing and operated in a continual flow of provisional miracles. Amazing things happened in his ministry. For instance, there was the widow woman who came to Elisha for help. Her husband had died, she couldn't pay her bills and her two sons were to be sold into slavery.

Her situation was serious. She needed provision, and asked the prophet what to do.

I like his response: "What do you have?"

What she had wasn't even a dime's worth of oil. But he sent her out to gather vessels to make provision for the increase she was about to receive. God miraculously increased her oil and it didn't stop pouring until she no longer had vessels to contain it.

Then Elisha told her to sell the oil, pay her bills, and she and her sons could live off the rest.

Her miracle was in her own house. An so is yours.

God will work a miracle with what you have, not with what you don't have. Just give Him what you have. He'll multiply it and keep it pouring as long as you have a place for Him to fill.

You may not have what you need, but you do have seed. The amount you have may not cover your bills, but you can sow something as seed for God to meet your need. You have what it takes to set your miracle in motion.

The whole kingdom of God works on farming principles. A farmer isn't going to run all over the community saying, "Would somebody please give me some corn." Of course not. He's going to take the corn he has, plow a field and plant his seed. And then the harvest will come.

The harvest you desire in your own life will come the same way—by seeding, not by pleading.

Miraculous Provision for the Harvest

The Church is standing on the verge of the greatest move of God to reach and rescue the souls of men that the earth has ever seen. To reap that kind of harvest will require the miracle power of God. But God isn't looking to pour out His power in places where the people will get stuck inside four walls because they can't afford to get out of town. What's the use in having a flow of physical miracles if you don't have the provision to take that power to people around the world? You can have power and you can have prayer, but if you don't have prosperity to propel you along, you won't get very far.

Recently, we were having a service and many Bible school graduates were in attendance. I asked, "How many of you are called to the nations?" Immediately, about 80 percent of the people in the room raised their hands. I thought, *Well, then why are you sitting here? You need to go. We love having you with us, but we'd rather you would be ministering on the mission field.*

Most of the people who acknowledged the calling on their lives that night didn't have the money to go and fulfill that call. But I'm telling you, those days are over. Some may hate the prosperity message, but

God loves it. And everywhere prosperity is preached, God will accompany and confirm that message with miraculous provision. Why? So He can send His Body out equipped to reach the nations!

The religious community gets fighting mad when you preach prosperity. But they don't realize that *GOD* is the One preaching prosperity. The reason is simple: In these last days God is looking to pour out His power on people who can afford to get that power out to a world that needs it.

The purpose for prosperity is not to take care of the Church. God can give us water out of a rock and feed us with manna from heaven. But He has to provide prosperity for the Church to reach the world. The world doesn't accept "manna" to fly airlines to the nations. They want dollars. So, since it takes dollars, God will give us dollars.

Provisional miracles. We must have them for this hour. It's no wonder John said, *"I [pray] above all things that thou mayest prosper..."* (3 John 2). Religion will fight prosperity to the end. But before it's all over, the Body of Christ will experience a flood of miracles. And that flood will begin with a tidal wave of provisional miracles and great prosperity.

This Gospel Must Be Preached

It's no wonder the devil has fought prosperity for so many years, because more people need a financial miracle than a physical miracle. That's because for 2,000 years the Church didn't have the backbone to preach prosperity . But this message must be preached. We're not going to reach the nations for God preaching a poverty message.

If you didn't preach salvation, how many people would get saved? If you didn't preach healing, how many people would get healed? Well, if you don't preach prosperity, how many people are going to walk in it and receive their needs met? You don't get the blessings of God without faith, you don't get faith without hearing, and you don't get hearing without preaching. And if somebody doesn't preach prosperity, people aren't going to have prosperity.

The Church will have to move in provisional miracles before we move into a flood of physical miracles. Then, God is going to unload some big dollars into the Church to help us reach the world and reap the harvest. Angels are working to bring the money in. And the time we have left before Jesus' return will be marked by notable miracles, many of provision.

Some people think the only people God will be able to use are those who have great business minds or who have had money behind them for generations. Not so. When God was ready to take care of the prophet in 1 Kings 17, He said first, "I've commanded a raven to take care of you." Then He said, "I've commanded an widow woman to take care of you."

You can be a bird, or even be broke, and God will use you! He's not looking for great ability. Just start out giving into the work of God. What you have is the seed of your miracle. Don't be surprised if God takes what you can do, and what you already have, and turns it into something a whole lot bigger than you can dream.

Think Like God—*BIG!*

Hanging around God and spending time with Him in the Word, in prayer and in fellowship with His Spirit will cause your spiritual capacity to increase. That's one reason why God is moving by His Spirit in this hour to get people filled and refilled with the Holy Ghost. Because the more you become filled to all fullness with God Himself, the more you think and act like Him. And God thinks BIG!

I started hanging around God so much that He stretched my vision and expectations further than I ever imagined possible. He's still stretching me. Today, we give as seed what we used to believe for as income.

I used to think if we preached from one end of the United States to the other, we'd really be doing something. Then when God dropped Europe in my heart—a continent of 750 million to a billion people—I thought that would keep us busy until halfway through the millennium. But recently God told me, *Expand the plan. What works in Europe will work in Asia.*

God thinks big. He has big plans. And it's going to take big dollars for us to put those plans into action.

That's why it's so important to be continually "being filled." The more full you become of God, the more you will think like Him. God is yanking the Church out of the confines of small, mediocre thinking because He has a big job for us to do. You may have a limited paycheck, but you don't have to have a limited income. You can have whatever you dare to believe. Let God expand your vision until your paycheck looks like seed for what He has for you down the road.

A poverty message is not going to reach and win the centers of the world, where the greatest harvest lies waiting for the Church. The gospel has never been bad news. The gospel of Jesus is good news. And good news to a poor person is that you don't have to be poor anymore!

God is pooling resources in preparation to reach the nations. He's finding people He can trust as His channels for provisional miracles. They are the men and women who will obey Him and give so He can multiply their investment.

God is going to dramatically multiply seed sown into the gospel. He does it with every other seed, certainly He can do it with financial seed. In fact, He must do it for the sake of the harvest. The nations of the world, the last great frontiers, are about to open up so the gospel can be preached to all the ends of the earth. Smith Wigglesworth said that before Jesus returns, the last part of the world to see a major move of God would be Australia, New Zealand and the islands of the sea. We're almost there.

So whatever it takes to get the job done— anointing, books, tapes, printed materials, aircraft, buildings—God will see to it that we have whatever we need to reach out and bring in that wonderful harvest.

Even if it takes a miracle.

The ABCs of Abundance

"(As it is written, I have made thee a father of many nations,) before him whom he believed, even God, who quickeneth the dead, and calleth those things which be not as though they were."
— ROMANS 4:17

Kenneth Copeland

Right now many of us are facing needs. Big needs. Needs so great that without the direct intervention of God, they can't possibly be met.

Because of that, we need to be more certain than ever before that we understand—and abide by—God's laws of abundance. Those laws are extremely important—but, praise God, they're not complicated. In fact, they're as simple as ABC.

A: Decide to Plant

In Mark 4, Jesus compared the workings of the kingdom of God to planting seeds in the earth. "When the seed is sown," He said, "it grows up and becomes greater" (verse 32).

Notice, He didn't say that when the seed is sown it occasionally grows up and becomes greater. Or it grows up and becomes greater if it's God's will. He said, "It grows up and becomes greater." Period.

God's economy isn't like ours. It isn't up one day and down the other. It's always the same and it always works perfectly. If you have good earth, good seed and good water, you will have growth. It's inevitable. The laws of God will produce that increase every single time.

So, if you're facing a need, don't panic— plant a seed!

That seed may take the form of money, time or some other resource you have to give. But no matter what form it takes, you need to understand that the gift itself isn't really your seed. There's no life in it. It's just the husk.

There are people who've planted husks for years. But, because they didn't put any life in them, nothing ever came up. So don't just plunk a husk in the offering bucket when it goes by. Put life in it first. Praise and worship God over it. Say, "Lord, I'm offering You my goods to do Your work with, and as I bring You my goods, I bring myself. I give myself to You, spirit, soul and body."

Pray over that seed. Fill it with faith, worship and the Word. Then it will be ready to plant.

B: Find Good Ground

Out in West Texas on my grandfather's farm, there were big, white patches of caliche. It's the most worthless dirt in the world when it comes to planting seed. It won't grow anything. I don't care how fine your seed is, if you plant it in caliche, you won't get a crop.

There are some ministries that, spiritually, are just like caliche. They aren't good ground for your seed. So before you give, pray about where that gift should go.

Don't rely on your own judgments. Don't reason it out and say, "Well, this preacher over here is screaming and crying and saying he's going under, so I guess I'll give to him." You go to the Lord of the tithe and find out where He wants you to put your money. He's the only One Who can direct you to truly good ground every time.

C: Water!

Once Your good seed is in good ground, keep watering it with the Word of God. Speak faith over it all week long. Call forth the growth of that seed by *"calling things that be not as though they were"* (Romans 4:17). It may just be a little seed, but you need to start calling it grown.

You may say, "Well, brother, I believe in telling things like they are."

You won't ever see any growth in your life then because spiritual things grow as words are released. That's God's way.

Charles Capps says the one who "tells things like they are" is like the guy who went out on the porch to give his dog a bone. When he got out there, he found the dog wasn't there—just the cat. So he started saying, "Here, kitty, kitty, kitty."

His neighbor said, "I thought you wanted to give that bone to the dog."

"I did," answered his friend, "but I like to say it like it is—and the cat, not the dog, is the one that's here."

Don't be like that guy. Call the dog. He'll come. Water your seed with words of faith. Don't call poverty if you don't want poverty. Call yourself prosperous. Call that need met. Before long, you'll be so full of joy and so full of expectancy that even the watering will be fun!

Plant the seed. Find good soil. Water it. Then as Mark 4:27 says, all you have to do is *"sleep, and rise night and day, and the seed will spring and grow up."*

"But I don't understand how that works!" you say.

It doesn't matter. Just do it. Plant and water. Sleep and rise. Sure enough, one of these mornings you'll wake up to an abundant harvest!

Why Is My Harvest So Small?

"Give, and it shall be given unto you; good measure, pressed down, and shaken together, and running over, shall men give into your bosom. For with the same measure that ye mete withal it shall be measured to you again."
— LUKE 6:38

Keith Moore

You can't figure it out. From the time you first learned about the principle of sowing and reaping, you have given offerings and sown seed into the kingdom of God. Although you've experienced a measure of blessing, you know you haven't reaped the thirty-, sixty-, hundredfold return Jesus said could be yours. Oftentimes you wonder, *Why is my harvest so small? I thought it would be bigger than this! What's wrong?*

There are reasons why people reap a small harvest. If your own harvests don't compare to the quality of increase you see in the Word of God, you can do something about that. The Bible gives us clear insights that, when followed, guarantee we will reap a plentiful harvest—every time.

Sow as Much as You Can

The first reason people only reap a small harvest can be found in 2 Corinthians 9:6: *"...He which soweth sparingly shall reap also sparingly; and he which soweth bountifully shall reap also bountifully."*

Jesus said, *"with the same measure that ye mete withal it shall be measured to you again"* (Luke 6:38).

That's such a basic principle, it seems obvious, but people overlook it. They'll put a dollar or two in the offering and when they don't receive much of a return they say, "I guess God just ordained me to have a small harvest." What they fail to realize is that God didn't determine the size of their harvest. They determined the size of their harvest the moment they decided how much seed to sow! If you don't sow much seed, you won't have much of a harvest.

"But, Brother Keith, I can't give any more than a few dollars," you say. "That's all I have!"

That's all right. Plant it and it will increase. Then take that increase and (instead of spending it on yourself) plant it again. You'll be amazed how fast it will grow.

I once read about a flour mill operator in Tecumseh, Mich., who experimented with this process. After hearing a sermon on the principles of sowing and reaping, he set aside one cubic inch of wheat, which is 360 kernels. Then he committed to the Lord that for six years, he would take the harvest from that ground, tithe 10 percent of it, and then sow the remaining 90 percent back into the ground.

The first year it took a 4-foot by 8-foot plot of ground to contain the harvest from that first cubic inch of wheat. The next year it took a 24-foot by 60-foot plot. By the sixth year, it took 2,666 acres because those first 360 kernels of wheat had multiplied to become 55 BILLION!

That testimony impacted me so strongly with the belief that, if you plant as much of your harvest back into the ground as you can, your harvests will increase until you'll have more than you could possibly eat. And you'll have much to give!

One big temptation people face, however, is when their harvest comes in, they want to spend it on themselves to immediately elevate their standard of living. They don't realize they're delaying their own prosperity by doing that. So don't eat your seed. Make giving a priority and then believe God to be able to give even more because *"A man's harvest in life will depend entirely on what he sows"* (Galatians 6:7, *New Testament in Modern English,* J.B. Phillips).

Sow Into Good Ground

The second reason people have small harvests is they don't sow their seed into good ground. Some ground is average.

Some ground is poor. Some is tremendous! The quantity of your harvest is directly affected by the quality of the ground where you have sown.

"How do I determine what is good ground?" you may ask.

First of all, Jesus said, *"Ye shall know them by their fruits"* (Matthew 7:16). If a ministry is yielding solid, scriptural fruit— such as getting people born again, edifying believers, preaching the unadulterated Word of God or helping the poor—then it's probably a good place to plant your seed.

Second, the Holy Spirit will not lead you to waste your seed by planting it in ground that's not strong and good enough to nourish it and produce a harvest. It's possible to waste seed by sowing money or things into certain people or works. That's why you need to be led by the Holy Spirit about where to and not to sow. Don't waste anything by haphazardly making decisions just off the top of your head. Listen. Stay open to the Spirit of God to direct your giving. Then follow that inward witness, knowing that He's leading you to sow in good ground.

Tithing Creates a Climate of Blessing

Natural seed needs the right amount of rain and sunshine to grow. The same is true of spiritual seed. It needs the blessing of God to produce a big harvest.

Tithing is the key to your harvest being blessed.

Although tithing does not qualify as sowing, it opens the windows of heaven and creates the right climate for your seed to flourish. Furthermore, if you're a tither, God says He will *"rebuke the devourer for your sakes, and he shall not destroy the fruits of your ground"* (Malachi 3:11).

Boll weevils, bugs and other insects will totally devour a crop. But you can be assured that when the devil sends spiritual bugs into your field, God Himself will say, *Get back, bugs! You can't eat that crop! It belongs to a tither. Because he puts Me first, I take care of him and his, personally!*

Discern Your Harvest

If you want to reap a bumper crop, in addition to planting plenty of seed, choosing good ground and creating a climate of blessing, you have another very important job to do. You have to discern when, where and how much or what size your harvest will be.

You probably have never thought about needing to discern your harvest. But that is why many of us have reaped only a little when we should have reaped a lot. We failed to discern our harvest!

Consider the importance of each of these elements, starting with the crucial element of timing. Scripturally, you know that you're not going to plant today and reap tomorrow. The Bible says we must wait until *"due season"* (Galatians 6:9). But the only way you can possibly tell when due season comes is by the witness of the Holy Spirit in your heart. First John 2:20 says, *"...ye have an unction [or anointing] from the Holy One, and ye know all things."* That unction will enable you to sense when you're getting close to your harvest.

One of the key indications that your harvest is due is that joy will rise up within you (see Isaiah 9:3). You'll have a sense of excitement in your heart. Your head may not be able to figure it out, but if you pay attention to what's inside you, you'll know that the time is near!

The Obedience of Faith

The next thing you need to know is where your harvest will be. Practically speaking, you have to locate where the cornfield is before you can reap the corn. The Lord knows that, and you can trust Him to help you find it.

But let me warn you, once He shows you where the field is, you'll have to take steps of faith to get to it. Romans 16:26 calls such steps the *"obedience of faith."* And if you don't take them, you won't receive the increase God has in store.

Read Luke 5 and you'll see that Peter faced that very situation. He sowed into Jesus' ministry by lending Him his boat and letting him preach from it. When Jesus was finished, He said to Peter, *"Launch out into the deep, and let down your nets for a draught"* (verse 4).

Peter was tired and hungry. He'd already fished all night without success. He knew there were no fish out there! What Jesus was actually doing was showing Peter where his harvest was. The problem was, now his nets were all washed and put away.

Peter had to take a step of faith to launch back out in that boat.

But, thank God, he took that step! If he hadn't, he would have missed his harvest. He would have missed the biggest catch of fish he'd ever seen in his life.

How many times have people tithed... and sowed...and waited? Then harvest time came and God said, *Take this step of expansion. Start this new business.* They were excited because they could see huge potential. But for whatever reason, they became afraid, yielded to unbelief and decided to play it safe. They didn't want to take on the extra contracts or do the necessary work.

As a result of not taking that step of obedience, they missed the blessings of God because they failed to discern their harvest. Their own lack of faith caused them to miss the place, the timing and the increase of harvest God had prepared for them.

Think BIG

When it comes to discerning your harvest, you also need to know the size of your harvest. When the Lord first spoke to me about this, He asked me a question. (I don't mean I heard a voice or saw a vision. I just knew in my heart what He was communicating to me.) *Keith,* He said, *do you know how much you sowed above your tithe last year?*

"Yes, Lord, I do," I answered. He had already taught me to be diligent to know the state of my flocks (see Proverbs 27:23).

He asked me further: *Have you thought about what even a fiftyfold return would be? Are you really expecting that much to come in?*

I whipped out the calculator, did the math and my eyes got big. It was a startlingly large figure! I had to say, "No, Lord. I'm not expecting that much."

Then stir up your faith! He said.

I don't mind telling you, I obeyed Him. And if you want to enjoy your full harvest, you should too because you don't just reap according to what you've sown, you reap according to your faith.

If your faith is smaller than your harvest, you'll be like the farmer who planted 500 acres, got a full crop, then went out and harvested only 50 acres. You'll end up leaving most of your crops in the field.

We have a big God. Make a decision to spend enough time in His Word that He can expand your "expecter"! Learn to think BIG, to claim BIG and to believe BIG THINGS. Then stay with it until your increase reflects the greatness of our God!

Keep on reaping...and reaping...and reaping...until you realize you have more than you can possibly use. Then call your brothers and sisters in the Lord and say, "Hey, let me give you some of what God has given me, I have plenty to spare!"

They'll be blessed. Your Heavenly Father will be well pleased. And you'll have more fun giving it away than you ever dreamed possible.

Now that's what I call a harvest!

What Happened to My Harvest?

"...Whatsoever a man soweth, that shall he also reap."
— GALATIANS 6:7

Keith Moore

It's frustrating. You've been confessing that God supplies all your needs, but you're still broke. What's even more puzzling is that you're a tither and a giver. You know that God's Word is true and He promised to open the windows of heaven and pour out blessings you wouldn't have room enough to receive. But...you still have plenty of room. You can't figure it out. You're wondering, *Where is my abundant supply? What happened to my harvest?*

When God began teaching me about the laws of increase, He showed me there are reasons why some people fail to reap a harvest and why others reap only a small one. If we'll give attention to those reasons— and make adjustments accordingly—we can enjoy a bumper crop of God's blessings every time!

First Things First

The first reason people fail to reap a harvest is simple and obvious. But we can't pass over it because it's the most common mistake people make.

When the Lord initially pointed it out to me, He said, *Keith, did you notice that I set up laws of sowing and reaping, not reaping and sowing?*

I realize that's very basic, but it's amazing how many people want to reap a harvest when they haven't even sown yet. Jesus said, *"Give, and it shall be given unto you"* (Luke 6:38). The Apostle Paul wrote, *"...he which soweth bountifully shall reap also bountifully"* (2 Corinthians 9:6). Again and again in the Scriptures, we see that sowing must come before reaping. Yet the number one reason why people fail to receive a harvest is because they haven't sown!

They'll make confessions. They'll turn in prayer requests. They'll call hot lines. But when all that is said and done the fact remains, if they haven't planted anything, if they haven't given anything, they're not going to reap a harvest.

"But Brother Keith," you may say, "I don't have anything to give!"

No problem. Second Corinthians 9:10 says God will provide seed for the sower. So if you have absolutely nothing, just say, "God, I need some seed to sow," and He'll give it to you.

When He does, don't just plant it haphazardly. Sow it in the particular area in which you want to reap. Here's why.

Genesis 1:11-12 plainly tells us that every seed produces after its own kind. That's not only true in the natural, it's true spiritually, too. Galatians 6:7 says it this way, *"Whatsoever a man soweth, that shall he also reap."* If you sow money, you'll reap money. If you sow jewelry, you'll reap jewelry. Whatever you sow is what will grow into a harvest in your life.

As soon as my wife and I started practicing this principle, things began to happen in our life. For example, we helped someone pay off their car. We made a payment for them every month for a year. Just a few months later, we were able to pay off our own car. We sowed a $3300 debt repayment and reaped a $15,000 debt repayment in return!

Right now you may be thinking, *That's great! I'll take part of my tithe and pay off someone's car!* If so, let me warn you: tithing is not sowing—there's a difference. When you tithe, you're giving back to God what already belongs to Him. The Bible says the firstfruits (that's the first and best 10 percent of your increase) belong to the Lord. Sowing implies giving something that belongs to you, so you're only sowing when you give something over and above your tithe.

Your tithe does affect your sowing, however. In fact, it's the key to your sowing being blessed. Malachi 3:10-13 says, when you tithe, God will open the windows of heaven, rain on the seed you've sown and multiply it many times over.

Don't Faint

The second reason why people don't reap is that they get tired of waiting for their harvest and give up. God warns us about that in Galatians 6:9. He tells us not to *"be weary in well doing: for in due season we shall reap, if we faint not."*

We have, however, a hard time waiting for "due season" because it almost always comes later than we want! Our flesh is impatient. It expects to plant a seed today and reap a harvest tomorrow. But that just doesn't happen.

Spiritual things work just like natural things. A farmer knows it will take a certain amount of time for his crop to grow. He doesn't try to rush the ground. He doesn't get on his tractor and drive around yelling, "Hurry up, crops. I need a harvest NOW!" He just waits patiently because he knows his harvest will come in due season.

Many charismatic Christians, on the other hand, seem to think that the moment they sow, the ground will quake, lightening will flash from the sky, and suddenly a massive harvest will shoot up from the ground. When that doesn't happen, they just shrug their shoulders and say, "Well, I guess I'm not going to get anything."

So they go on about their business and never give another thought to the seed they planted. As a result, they faint and miss their due season by forgetting what and where they sowed. Many times this happens because people don't take their giving seriously enough to even expect a harvest. They view their giving as a loss instead of as an investment.

Take your sowing seriously. Remember when and where you planted seed. Every time you think about it say, "I've sown in that area and I'm expecting a harvest!" Then constantly watch for it. Proverbs 10:5 says, *"He that gathereth in summer is a wise son: but he that sleepeth in harvest is a son that causeth shame."* Don't be a sleeping son at harvest time. Stay awake and reap the rewards!

Reaping Is NOT Automatic

"If I plant good seed in faith, won't my harvest just automatically come in?"

No. It won't. Reaping is no more automatic than sowing. Read the parable Jesus told in Mark 4 and you'll see what I mean:

...So is the kingdom of God, as if a man should cast seed into the ground; And should sleep, and rise night and day, and the seed should spring and grow up, he knoweth not how. For the earth bringeth forth fruit of herself; first the blade, then the ear, after that the full corn in the ear. But when the fruit is brought forth, immediately he putteth in the sickle, because the harvest is come (verses 26-29).

God didn't sow the seed in this parable. The man did. God gave the increase. Then it was the man who reaped the harvest by putting in the sickle.

Reaping takes work. It requires action on our part. Just as a farmer doesn't sit around at harvest time expecting his crops to march out of the field and into the barn all by themselves, we cannot expect our harvest to come in without our help. Maybe you

were hoping God would take the responsibility for it all. But He won't.

If you'll read the Bible, you'll see that
even when God supplied spectacular,
miraculous provision, He still required His
people to go out and gather it. When the
Israelites were in the wilderness, for
instance, God poured food down on them
from the sky. But they couldn't just sit in
their tents and wait. It fell in little flakes
like snow and they had to take their pot
and pick up these little specks until they
had collected enough to make bread. They
had to reap the harvest!

Spiritually speaking, you will have to do
the same thing. You have to thrust in your
sickle of faith and lay claim to the provision
that's yours by right of the seed you've sown.
You have to say, "I believe I receive my
harvest in Jesus' Name. Now go, ministering
spirits, and cause my money (or whatever it
is) to come in!" (see Hebrews 1:14).

In other words, you must reap by faith
just like you sow by faith. Instead of just
sitting around "waiting on the Lord," you

must become aggressive. You have to go after what's yours.

Mark 11:24 tells us how to do that. It says, *"What things soever ye desire, when ye pray, believe that ye receive them, and ye shall have them."*

Look again at that verse. It says you're to believe. Believe what? Believe that you receive.

It's not enough for you to believe God is good and wants you to prosper. It's not enough for you to believe that your harvest is out there. You must believe that you receive. In this passage, the word translated *receive* literally means "take." You can't be a timid soul and be successful in the Christian life. The Apostle Paul told Timothy, *"Fight the good fight of faith, lay hold on eternal life..."* (1 Timothy 6:12). When it comes to enjoying the blessings of God that are provided for you, you have to wade in and lay hold—you have to be bold to possess what God said belongs to you.

So get busy. Plant some seed in the specific area where you need a harvest. Stand strong, stay alert and awake until due season comes.

Then put in the sickle and take what God has given you.

Faithful Over Little— Ruler Over Much

"Well done, thou good and faithful servant: thou hast been faithful over a few things, I will make thee ruler over many things: enter thou into the joy of thy lord."
— MATTHEW 25:21

Gloria
Copeland

You may not realize it, but if you're a born-again believer, you have a quality within you that is in great demand in the world today.

It's a quality employers prize so highly that they'll promote people who have it— and often pay top dollar for it. It's a quality so valuable it can make you a success in every area of your life.

What one quality could possibly be so precious?

The quality of faithfulness.

According to the dictionary, *faithfulness* is "firmly adhering to duty, of true fidelity

or loyalty, true allegiance, constant in performance of duties or services." A faithful person
is   steadfast,   dependable   and   trustworthy. He's consistent.

A faithful person keeps his word. When
he says he'll do a job, you can count on him
to get it done and done well. If he is being
paid by the hour, he doesn't steal from his
employer by wasting his time. He works
diligently even when his boss isn't watching. He's honorable, treating others with
the same kindness and integrity with which
he would like to be treated.

Spiritually, a faithful person is exactly
what that word implies—full of faith. He
trusts consistently in the Word of God and
acts consistently on that Word. He doesn't
have faith in God one moment and doubt
Him the next. He steadily believes God and
does what He says.

"Certainly faithfulness is a wonderful
quality," you may say. "But I have to be
honest. I just don't have it!"

You do if you have made Jesus the Lord
of your life and been born again. Because

Galatians 5:22 says, *"...the fruit of the Spirit is love, joy, peace, patience, kindness, goodness, faithfulness, gentleness and self-control" (New International Version)*. That's the fruit of your reborn spirit.

When you were born again, God re-created your spirit in His own image. He put His own character within you, and one of God's most outstanding character traits is His faithfulness. As 1 Corinthians 1:9 says, *"God is faithful—reliable, trustworthy and [therefore] ever true to His promise, and He can be depended on" (The Amplified Bible)*.

Actually, the kind of faithfulness God has put within us is more than just a character trait. It's a supernatural force that comes to our rescue in times of trouble. It gives us the ability to keep going when things get tough.

The force of faithfulness is what enables us to continue living by faith even when our fleshly inclination is to throw down the Bible and say, "I quit!" It's the force that causes us to go to work, and smile, and do our best—even on days when we'd rather stay in bed.

The Sure Path to Promotion

Of course, even though the supernatural force of faithfulness is within you, for it to operate in your life, you have to yield to it. You have to develop it and exercise it. But it's worth the effort because the Bible promises that the *"faithful man shall abound with blessings!"* (Proverbs 28:20).

That holds true in every area of life. When you're faithful spiritually, you abound with spiritual blessings and that opens the door for blessings in every other area. When you're faithful on your job, you abound with financial blessings. When you're faithful at home, you're blessed with a good, strong family.

What's more, Jesus told us that those who would be faithful over little would be made ruler over much (see Matthew 25:21). So faithfulness is a sure path to promotion!

Employers, for instance, are desperate for faithful people. The world is full of employees who will just do enough to keep from getting fired. It's full of people who will slack off the moment the boss isn't looking. It's full of people who may come to work—and may not. That's how worldly people are!

But it's a treasure for employers to find a person who works wholeheartedly at his job, who is trustworthy and dependable and honest. So when an employer finds a person like that, he's usually eager to promote him.

The fact is, every believer ought to be that kind of person. Each one of us should live a lifestyle of faithfulness. As Ken says, in every situation we should make it a lifestyle to do what's right, do it because it's right and do it right. Anything less is disobedience to God's Word.

In the work place, we should be following the instructions in Colossians 3:22-24:

> **Servants, obey in everything those who are your earthly masters, not only when their eyes are on you, as pleasers of men, but in simplicity of purpose (with all your heart) because of your reverence for the Lord and as a sincere expression of your devotion to Him. Whatever may be your**

task, work at it heartily (from the soul), as [something done] for the Lord and not for men, Knowing (with all certainty) that it is from the Lord [and not from men] that you will receive the inheritance which is your (real) reward. [The One Whom] you are actually serving [is] the Lord Christ, the Messiah *(The Amplified Bible)*.

Ken and I have seen some of the employees at this ministry take that attitude and, as a result, be promoted again and again. One man started out with the simple job of duplicating tapes for us, but over the years he was so faithful that he eventually became director over the business affairs of the entire ministry.

You may think, *Well, that wouldn't work in my case. My boss is an unfair man. He wouldn't reward my faithfulness.*

That's no problem. The scripture doesn't say your reward will come from your employer. It says your reward will come from the Lord!

You see, God has established a principle of sowing and reaping in the earth—and that principle is always at work. As Galatians 6:7 says, *"Be not deceived; God is not mocked: for whatsoever a man soweth, that shall he also reap."* If you plant faithfulness in your job, you will receive blessing in return—even if that blessing means a different but better job. Granted, that blessing may not come overnight, but if you will not be weary in well doing, in due season you shall reap, if you faint not (verse 8).

So make up your mind to put your whole heart into your work, no matter how menial or unpleasant it may seem to be. Do it well. Do it with a smile and an attitude of enthusiasm and say, "Lord, You know this is not where I want to be. But I am sowing faithfulness into this job as seed for a better job." I guarantee you, a better job will soon come along.

Recently, the Lord has impressed me that it is important for us as believers to obey these principles of faithfulness right now, especially in the area of finances and employment. Why is that? I'm not sure. I don't know what is going to happen to the economy of this world between now and the time Jesus catches us away. But there may come a time when jobs are more scarce than they are now. If so, we'll definitely want to be reaping the blessings of faithfulness. And we can be, if we'll start sowing right now. Besides that, it's the right thing to do!

Lions Don't Eat Faithful Men

Some Christians get nervous when they hear things like that. It scares them to think that difficult times might be ahead. But it shouldn't, because Psalm 31:23 tells us *"the Lord preserveth the faithful."*

It doesn't matter how dark the world around us may become. It doesn't matter how hard the devil tries to bring us down, if we're steadfast, dependable and trustworthy—constantly serving the Lord and doing what's right—God will bring us through in victory.

If you have any question about that, just take a look at what He did in the life of Daniel. When Daniel was just a young man, his nation was besieged and defeated by the nation of Babylon. He was taken captive from his own country and brought to serve in the palace of the Babylonian king.

Even though Daniel was an alien in Babylon, he was eventually promoted to one of the highest positions in the nation. He served as one of three presidents directly under the king himself. Daniel did his job so faithfully that he *was preferred above the presidents and princes, because an excellent spirit was in him; and the king thought to set him over the whole realm"* (Daniel 6:3).

When the other presidents and princes found out that Daniel was about to be promoted and given power over them, they were jealous. So they looked for some accusation to bring against him.

You know how it is at election time. Each candidate tries to find something bad they can say about the other. Sometimes, they don't have to look too hard, either.

In Daniel's case, however, it was different. His opponents *"could find none occasion nor fault; forasmuch as he was faithful, neither was there any error or fault found in him. Then said these men, We shall not find any occasion against this Daniel, except we find it against him concerning the law of his God"* (verses 4-5).

They couldn't dig up any real dirt on Daniel, so they came up with a scheme to trap him. Since he was faithful to God and prayed every day, they talked the king into signing a decree *"that whosoever shall ask a petition of any God or man for thirty days, save of [the]...king, he shall be cast into the den of lions"* (verse 7).

Do you know what Daniel did when he heard about that decree? The same thing he had always done. He just kept on being faithful. *"...he went into his house; and his windows being open in his chamber toward Jerusalem, he kneeled upon his knees three times a day, and prayed, and gave thanks before his God..."* (verse 10).

Of course, Daniel's opponents immediately informed the king that Daniel had broken the law and must be thrown to the lions. The king was grieved and tried to figure out a way to deliver Daniel from his death sentence. But because the king himself had signed the law, it could not be changed.

As they cast Daniel into the den of lions, the king said to him:

> ...Thy God whom thou servest continually, he will deliver thee... Then the king went to his palace, and passed the night fasting...and his sleep went from him. Then the king arose very early in the morning, and went in haste unto the den of lions. And when he came to the den, he cried with a lamentable voice unto Daniel: and the king spake and said...O Daniel, servant of the living God, is thy God, whom thou servest continually, able to deliver thee from the lions? (verses 16, 18-20).

Notice that both times the king spoke to Daniel, he mentioned the fact that Daniel continually served God. In other words, what stood out about Daniel was his faithfulness. He spiritually wasn't up one day, and down the next. He wasn't believing God on Sunday and then crying on Monday about how depressed he was. He was faithful—both in spiritual things and in natural things.

So what happened? God preserved him! God sent His angel and shut the lions' mouths so they couldn't hurt him. Just think, Daniel slept better in the lions' den that night than the king did in the palace!

The next morning, the king brought Daniel out of the lions' den and then commanded that his accusers be thrown in it along with their families. The lions devoured them before they hit the floor. After all, they had missed dinner the night before!

That just goes to show you, it never pays to try to destroy a faithful man. If you do, you'll end up being destroyed yourself—and he'll end up not just being preserved, but being promoted.

That's what happened to Daniel. He *"prospered in the reign of Darius, and in the reign of Cyrus the Persian"* (verse 28).

He went through these two kings and was abundantly blessed under both of them.

Make a Change!

Will God do for you what He did for Daniel? He certainly will! Jesus left no question about that for He said: *"Who then is a faithful and wise servant, whom his lord hath made ruler over his household, to give them meat in due season? Blessed is that servant, whom his lord when he cometh shall find so doing. Verily I say unto you, That he shall make him ruler over all his goods"* (Matthew 24:45-47).

God gives us certain responsibilities in His kingdom. He gives us assignments. Our first assignment might be nothing more than to weed the flower bed at the church or to wait tables at a restaurant. But if we'll be faithful over that assignment, the next assignment He gives us will be bigger and better.

So start being faithful with what God has given you right now. Be faithful spiritually by diligently attending to the Word every day. Follow the instructions in Proverbs 4 and let

God's Word *"not depart from thine eyes; keep them in the midst of thine heart...Keep thy heart with all diligence; for out of it are the issues of life"* (verses 21, 23).

Put yourself in position to increase in the natural realm by being faithful with the material things God has given you. For example, if you're living in a rent house and you want a house of your own, treat that rent house as if it belonged to you. Don't tear it up and be careless with it. For Jesus said, *"...if ye have not been faithful in that which is another man's, who shall give you that which is your own?"* (Luke 16:12).

Until now, you may have acted like the most unfaithful person around. You may feel like you've made disastrous mistakes in your life by being been undependable and untrustworthy. You may have always been a quitter. But you can start changing that today because as a child of God, you have inside you His very own force of faithfulness. So start yielding to it.

Begin to strengthen that force by meditating on God's Word. Read and study what it says about faithfulness. Since faith comes by hearing, and hearing by the Word of God, you can build your ability to believe you are faithful by turning your attention away from who you've been in the past, and focusing instead on who the Word says you are today.

And who does the Word say you are today?

It says you are among those who have sided with Jesus. You can be among those who *"are called, and chosen, and faithful!"* (Revelation 17:14). The Holy Spirit will help you.

Remind the devil of that next time he pressures you to quit. Remind him of it when he tempts you to do less than your best. Then determine to be the kind of person God can trust to follow through, no matter what the inconvenience or discomfort. Say, "Lord, I am a faithful person. I will get my job done and do it well. I will trust You to help me, energize me and create in me the power and desire. And I'll stay with it at any cost."

Step out in faithfulness and you shall abound with blessings!

Do You Know What Time It Is?

Chapter 14

"Now unto him that is able to do exceeding abundantly above all that we ask or think, according to the power that worketh in us."
— EPHESIANS 3:20

Gloria
Copeland

If you're a born-again child of God and you've been struggling financially— scraping along with just barely enough— it's time for that to change. It's time for you to wake up to the riches that belong to you in Jesus, kick the limits off your faith and receive your financial inheritance.

Even if you haven't been struggling, even if your bills are paid and your major needs are met, you need to step up to greater abundance. We all need to do that, because God has more in store for every one of us than we possess right now. He *"is able to do exceeding abundantly above all that we ask or think, according to the power that worketh in us"* (Ephesians 3:20).

What's more, we are now closer than ever to the end of the age. Jesus is coming soon. God is desiring to pour out His glory in greater measure than ever before, not just in our hearts, lives and church services, but in our finances as well.

Some time ago, the Lord began to speak to me about that. *Do you know what time it is?* He said. *It's exceeding-abundantly-above-all-that-you-can-ask-or-think time!*

I don't mind telling you, I was thrilled when I heard those words! And I've gotten even more excited about them as the months have passed, because the Holy Spirit has continued to say them to me. I believe it, too! I believe it with all my heart!!

We are in the days of the end-time transfer of wealth about which the Bible prophesies. In these days, God is teaching us how to draw great riches from our heavenly account so we can glorify Him and get the gospel preached to the world. He is revealing to us how we can have more than enough to give to every good work and have plenty left over to enjoy!

God's Financial Safeguard

The very idea of that kind of wealth scares some Christians. They think having a lot of money is ungodly—but that's not what the Bible says.

God doesn't object to us having money. On the contrary, He *"takes pleasure in the prosperity of His servant"* (Psalm 35:27, *The Amplified Bible*). What God doesn't want us to do is covet money. He doesn't want us to love money and make it our God.

So He gave us a safeguard. He gave us in His Word a foundational instruction about prosperity that enables us to be wealthy and godly at the same time. *"Seek for (aim at and strive after) first of all His [God's] kingdom, and His righteousness [His way of doing and being right], and then all these things taken together will be given you besides"* (Matthew 6:33, *The Amplified Bible*).

That is the foundation of biblical prosperity. It's based on God's way of doing and being right. It comes to those who operate in this earth according to His system of economy instead of the world's system.

The world's system has money for its god. It loves and seeks after money. But the kingdom of heaven has the Father for its God. And in His economy, you can't prosper unless you put Him and His ways first place in your life.

Granted, there are times when godly people begin to prosper and then get off track. Those people pass the poverty test, but fail the prosperity test. They start out seeking first God's kingdom. But when they begin to experience the financial blessings of that kingdom, they become overly occupied with the things that have been added to them. Their hearts begin to grow cold toward God because they don't continue to give Him first place in their lives.

God doesn't want that to happen to His people. That's why He told the Israelites not to forget Him when they entered the Promised Land, started living in goodly houses and enjoying material abundance. *"But you shall (earnestly) remember the Lord your God; for it is He Who gives you power to get wealth..."* (Deuteronomy 8:18, *The Amplified Bible*).

Your Heavenly Account

Notice God didn't say, "Since you might forget Me if you get rich, I'm going to keep you poor." No, He said, "Always remember that I'm the One Who gives you the power to get wealth." Remember where you got it!

Hallelujah! As born-again believers, you and I are God's people just as surely as those Israelites were. Since we are Christ's, then we are *"Abraham's seed, and heirs according to the promise"* (Galatians 3:29). Therefore, we can expect God to anoint the work of our hands. We can expect Him to bless us and give us the power to get wealth!

"But Gloria," you may say, "I know people who have served God and put Him first all their lives, yet, they were always broke. God didn't give them the power to get wealth!"

Yes, He did. They just didn't know how to use it.

You see, God's abundance doesn't just fall out of heaven and hit us on the head. He has designated ways for us to receive it.

179

If we don't know how to operate in those ways, we will miss out on what is ours.

That's really not surprising when you think about it. Even things on earth work that way. For example, you can have a million dollars in a bank account, but if you don't know it's there or if you don't know how to make a withdrawal on your account, you won't be able to enjoy that money.

The same thing is true in the kingdom of God. The Bible says you have a heavenly account. The Apostle Paul referred to it when he wrote to his partners and thanked them for giving into his ministry. *"Not because I desire a gift,"* he said, *"but I desire fruit that may abound to your account"* (Philippians 4:17).

Your heavenly account is much like an earthly bank account in that you can make deposits in it. Not only is it possible to make deposits there, Jesus told us it is very important for us to do so. In Matthew 6:19-21, He said: *"Lay not up for yourselves treasure upon earth, where moth and rust doth corrupt, and where thieves break through and steal: But lay up for yourselves treasures in heaven, where neither moth nor rust doth corrupt, and where thieves do not break through nor steal: For where your treasure is, there will your heart be also."*

It's a wonderful thing to have an account in heaven! It's a wonderful thing to know like Paul's partners did, that *"...God will liberally supply (fill to the full) your every need according to His riches in glory in Christ Jesus"* (Philippians 4:19, *The Amplified Bible*).

Headquarters for heaven's economy is not in the impoverished system of this world, but in glory! The government of heaven has for its source El Shaddai, the One Who is more than enough!

That's good news because the governments of this world are, for the most part, broke. They print money that doesn't have gold to back it up. They borrow money from other governments. They even borrow it from you.

But God doesn't have to print money He can't back up. His streets are gold. He owns everything. God has the greatest real estate conglomerate that ever existed. He has a lot of land leased out, but He can repossess it whenever He wants.

That's what He did for the nation of Israel. He repossessed the land of Canaan, the Promised Land, from the wicked. He said to the Israelites, "Here, you can have this land. I'm giving it to you. All you have to do is go in there and take it." (Other times, He told them they couldn't have certain places because He had already given it to "so-and-so.")

Think about that! The Canaanites had dug wells and built houses on that land. But God gave it away right out from under them. He had a right to do it. It all belonged to Him. As Psalm 50:10 says, *He* owns *"the cattle upon a thousand hills."* ("And the 'taters under them, too!" as one fellow added.)

The Bottom Line

Once you understand you have a heavenly account into which you can make deposits, the next question you need to answer is this: How do I make those deposits?

You make them by giving to God's work.

The foundation for that giving is the tithe. When you give the first tenth of your income to the Lord, you open the door for God to come into your finances and move supernaturally. Proverbs 3:10 says that when you honor the Lord with the firstfruits of your increase, *"so shall your storage places be filled with plenty"* (The Amplified Bible).

In addition to your tithe, you can also deposit to your heavenly account by giving offerings into the work of the gospel. Be sure, however, when you give, you are truly giving into a work of God. You have to put your money in good ground if you want to get a return.

If you're like me, you're already getting eager to get to the bottom line here. You're saying, "OK, I know that I have an account. I know where it is, and I know how to make deposits. But when can I get the money? When can I write a check on this account?"

You find the answer to that question in Mark 10:29-30. There, Jesus was answering the disciples who had asked Him what they were going to get in return for the giving they had done for the gospel's sake. He said: *"Verily I say unto you, There is no man that hath left house, or brethren, or sisters, or father, or mother, or wife, or children, or lands, for my sake, and the gospel's, But he shall receive an hundredfold now in this time, houses, and brethren, and sisters, and mothers, and children, and lands, with persecutions; and in the world to come eternal life."*

Jesus says we can receive a hundredfold return from our heavenly account today, in this time! Although our deposits are going to be bringing us rewards for eternity, we don't have to wait until we die and go to heaven to draw on those resources. We can make withdrawals on our heavenly account here and now!

Don't Let Tradition Cheat You

How do you make those withdrawals? You make them by faith. You believe in your heart and speak with your mouth that "My God supplies all my need according to His riches in glory by Christ Jesus" (Philippians 4:19).

You reach out with the hand of faith and claim what's yours!

Many Christians seem reluctant to do that. They remind me of the elder brother in the story of the prodigal son. Do you remember him? His younger brother had asked for his share of the inheritance, so the boys' father divided his estate between them.

The younger brother ran off and squandered his share of the estate on a sinful lifestyle. The elder brother stayed home and faithfully served his father. When the younger brother repented and returned home asking only to be treated as a servant in his father's house, the father received him with open arms. He killed a calf for him so they could celebrate with a feast. He put a robe on his back and a ring on his finger.

The older brother was furious and said to his father, *"Lo, these many years do I serve thee, neither transgressed I at any time thy commandment: and yet thou never gavest me a kid, that I might make merry with my friends: But as soon as this thy son was come, which hath devoured thy living with harlots, thou hast killed for him the fatted calf"* (Luke 15:29-30).

The father's answer is very important to us and we need to consider it carefully. He said, *"Son, thou art ever with me, and all that I have is thine"* (verse 31).

That father had divided his estate between his two boys. Therefore, after the younger brother had taken his goods and departed, everything that was left belonged to the elder son. Everything! He could have eaten a fatted calf every day if he'd wanted. Every cow on the estate belonged to him, but he didn't take advantage of his inheritance!

A multitude of Christians are going to find themselves in the same situation when they get to heaven. They're going to find out after they get there what belonged to them down here. They're going to realize too late that they were cheated and swindled out of their earthly inheritance by religious tradition.

They're going to find out then what you are finding out right now, and it's this: God has always wanted His people to live in abundance, and all He has is ours. He put every good thing in this earth for His family. He didn't put riches here for the devil and his family. He put them here for us.

God wants you to live in a good house. He wants you to have the car you need. He wants you to be so blessed you don't even have to think about those things. He wants you to be able to think about Him instead of thinking about how you're going to buy your next tank of gas.

Listen, God isn't anywhere near broke! He has enough wealth to richly supply all of His children. Lack is not His problem. His problem has been getting His people to believe what He says about their prosperity in His Word. His problem has been getting us to be kingdom-of-God minded in our finances.

God's Hand Is Not Short

One thing that has kept us from becoming kingdom-of-God minded is our own human reasoning. Instead of just trusting God to do for us what He promised, we try to figure out how He is going to do it. And if we can't see how it can happen, all too often, we won't believe.

Don't do that. Get out beyond what you can reason. God is not reasonable! Don't base your praying and your faith on what you can see in this natural realm. Base your praying and your faith on what the Word says.

For example, stop being content just to believe God for the money to make your house payment each month. Start believing Him for the money to pay off the entire mortgage!

"But, Gloria, I just don't know how God would ever get that kind of money to me."

So what! Moses didn't know how God was going to bring in enough meat to feed over a million Israelites for a month, either. So when God said He was going to do it, Moses said, "It would take all our herds and flocks to feed this bunch! It would take all the fish in the sea! It's impossible!"

"And the Lord said unto Moses, Is the Lord's hand waxed short?" (Numbers 11:23).

Then He proved He was able to do what He said by raining so much quail out of heaven the Israelites actually got sick of it!

When you have a need in your life that seems impossible to meet, think about that. Remember the question God asked Moses. *"Is the Lord's hand waxed short?"*

No! It wasn't short then and it isn't short now. God knows how to get the job done. He knows how to get you everything you need. So look to Him as your Source. Become expectant. Become miracle minded, blessing minded, supernatural increase minded.

God knows how to do things. You don't have to worry about that. You just focus on your part—believe, speak the Word and walk in the ways of God. Stop limiting God just because you don't understand how He is going to do the things He has promised. If we had to depend on what we could understand, we'd be in great trouble. But we don't! All we have to understand is that God is God and He has all power. He is able to do exceeding, abundantly above all we can ask or think!

That means if you can think of it, God is able to do more than that. If you can dream of it, God is able to do more than that. If you can hope for it, God is able to do more than that.

Whatever needs or godly desires you might have, God is able to satisfy them— and then do much, much more. And as I said before, these are the days when we will see that superabundance. This is the time.

"What time is it?" you ask.

IT'S EXCEEDING-ABUNDANTLY-ABOVE-ALL-YOU-CAN-ASK-OR-THINK TIME!

I plan to make the most of it. Don't you?

How to Prosper From the Inside Out

"Beloved, I wish above all things that thou mayest prosper and be in health, even as thy soul prospereth."
— 3 JOHN 2

Kenneth Copeland

Whether they admit it or not, a great many believers have trouble believing—really believing—they'll ever be financially prosperous. You can show them what the Word of God says. You can load them up with scriptures that prove God's will for them is prosperity—and they'll agree with every word. But they'll still go home and live poor. When they look around them at their mountains of bills, the faltering economy, and their dead-end job, they just can't see how God could possibly prosper them. *After all, what's He going to do?* they wonder. *Start floating twenty dollar bills down from the trees?*

How does God prosper His people? It's a good question. One that deserves an answer, and you can find it in 3 John 2. There the elder Apostle John writes by inspiration of the Holy Ghost: *"Beloved, I wish above all things that thou mayest prosper and be in health, even as thy soul prospereth."*

I want you to notice something. That scripture doesn't say I pray you prosper even as the economy prospers or even as your employer decides to promote you. It says I pray you prosper as your soul prospers.

That's where most believers miss it when it comes to receiving financial prosperity. They keep looking at situations outside them, thinking that's where their hope lies. But God doesn't work from the outside in. He works from the inside out.

He blesses you materially as your soul prospers on His Word. Then, as the seeds of prosperity are planted in your mind, in your will and in your emotions, and as you allow those seeds to grow, they eventually produce a great financial harvest—no matter how bad the conditions around you may be.

Read the story of Joseph in Genesis 37 through 41 and you can see exactly what I'm talking about. When Joseph was sold as a slave to the Egyptians, he didn't have a dime to his name. He didn't even have his freedom. But, right in the middle of his slavery, God gave Joseph such wisdom and ability that he made his owner, Potiphar, rich. As a result, Potiphar put Joseph in charge of all his possessions.

Later, Potiphar's wife got mad at Joseph and he ended up in prison. Talk about a dead-end job! There's really not much chance for advancement in prison, is there? But God gave him insight that no other man in Egypt had. He gave him such great wisdom that he ended up on Pharaoh's staff—not as a slave but as the most honored man in the entire country next to Pharaoh himself. From prison to prime minister.

He rode along in a chariot and people literally bowed down before him. During a worldwide famine, Joseph was in charge of all the food. Now that's prosperity!

How did God accomplish that? By prospering Joseph's soul. No matter how dismal Joseph's situation became, no matter how impossible his problems, God was able to reveal the spiritual secrets that would open the door of success for him.

That's what makes God's method of prospering so exciting. It works anywhere and everywhere. It will work in the poorest countries on the face of this earth just like it will work here in the United States. I've seen it happen.

A few years ago, for instance, we received an amazing firsthand report from an African village called Rungai. I'll never forget the story. There had been such a long drought in the countryside surrounding Rungai that the village was in terrible shape. The reservoir that had once supplied it with water had been empty for so long that the dam was broken and crumbling.

There didn't seem to be any hope. Then a local pastor latched onto God's Word concerning prosperity. He began to pray and seek God's guidance. Sure enough, it came.

God told him to get the believers in the village together and rebuild the dam. I'm sure it looked like a ridiculous thing to do. There hadn't been any rain for months and there wasn't a cloud in the sky. But God had given them the secret to success and, in faith obedience, they acted on it.

Not long after the job was done, a rain cloud formed right over their little reservoir, filling it with water. But that's not the end of the story.

You see, the soil at Rungai had been so parched, so full of alkali and poison, that nothing much would grow in it. Yet, after that rain, the pastor called all the people together and told them to start planting around that water hole. He knew God was going to prosper those crops. He also knew that the crops belonging to the believers would be especially blessed. So when he parceled out the land, he interspersed the believers' plots among those of the unbelievers so that the miracle of God could be clearly seen.

During that first season, everybody's crops flourished. Sinners and believers alike. Then the season for harvesting ended. All the sinners' crops died as they were supposed to. But all the believers' crops produced another harvest. Then another. Then another. The believers' crops just kept producing all year long.

Now you may say, "Brother Copeland, God did more than just prosper their souls there. He worked some miracles."

Yes, He did. But how much good would those miracles have done if He hadn't prospered that pastor's soul first? How much good would that rain have been if the pastor hadn't heard from God and patched up the dam before it came? How much good would it have done for God to bless the soil if that pastor hadn't heard God's instructions to plant there?

Those miracles wouldn't have helped those people one bit if God hadn't prospered their souls first! It was because they believed His Word and were willing to listen to His voice that He could reveal to them the secrets of success for their particular situation.

Deuteronomy 29:29 says this: *"The secret things belong unto the LORD our God: but those things which are revealed belong unto us and to our children for ever, that we may do all the words of this law."*

Secret things! How many times have you racked your brain, trying to figure out the solution to a problem? You knew there was an answer, but you just couldn't figure out what it was. In other words, the answer was a secret—a secret that only God knew. It didn't belong to you.

But if you'd gone to the Word and really searched it in prayer and meditation, that secret would have been revealed! God would have shown you precisely what the solution to that problem was.

In Mark 4:21-22, Jesus says, *"Is a candle brought to be put under a bushel, or under a bed? and not to be set on a candlestick? For there is nothing hid, which shall not be manifested; neither was any thing kept secret, but that it should come abroad."*

God doesn't want you groping around in the dark. He wants to reveal His secrets to you, secrets that will prosper you and make you successful in every area of your life—including your finances.

That's why He's given you the Holy Spirit. Do you have any idea what a tremendous resource He is? Most believers don't. They get in church and say, "Oh, yes, amen, brother. Thank God for the Holy Spirit. Praise God. Hallelujah." Then they go home and forget about Him.

It's not that they aren't sincere on Sunday. They are. They genuinely appreciate the little bit they understand about the Holy Spirit. But they haven't learned how to tap into the unlimited wisdom and power He can make available to them in their daily lives.

Jesus said, *"Howbeit when he, the Spirit of truth, is come, he will guide you into all truth: for he shall not speak of himself; but whatsoever he shall hear, that shall he speak: and he will show you things to come"* (John 16:13).

Read that verse again and think about it.

Jesus said the Holy Spirit would guide us into all truth! Not just enough truth to get by on. Not just an occasional truth to help us teach our Sunday school classes. All truth!

If you're a businessman, that means the Holy Spirit will show you how to increase your profits and reduce your expenses. If you're a mother, it means the Holy Spirit will show you how to settle arguments between your children. If you're a student, it means the Holy Spirit will show you how to excel in your classes.

In fact, if you know Jesus Christ as your Lord and are baptized in the Holy Spirit, somehow inside you is the answer to every financial problem, every spiritual problem, and every physical problem that exists. You have answers for problems you don't even know about yet.

There's a story that came out of World War II that illustrates that perfectly. The United States Navy had run into some serious trouble. Their ships were being sunk by the enemy faster than they could build new ones, a process which at the time took an entire year.

Finally, they came up with a way that made it possible to build a ship in a single day. But there was one hitch. The process involved building the ship upside down and when the ships were turned upright, the welds would pop and the ship would come apart.

The problem was presented to a deeply spiritual man who was a famous industrialist at the time. "I'll find out how to do it," he said. After days of prayer and fasting, God showed him the welding formula that would hold the ship together.

One idea! Just one idea made it possible to go from building a ship a year, to building a ship a day.

Can you begin to see now how God could prosper you?

There are so many people standing around wringing their hands and worrying. "God could never prosper me," they say. "All I get is this little paycheck...and my company's losing money, so I know they're not going to give me a raise. How on earth is God going to prosper me?"

Maybe He'll give you an idea that will take your company's loss and turn it into a profit. Maybe He'll give you an idea for a new product and you'll start your own company.

God has probably already given you idea after idea that would have made you rich if you'd just had spiritual sense enough to recognize them. But you didn't even know they were there because you weren't paying attention to the things of God. You weren't seeking revelations of the "secret things." You were probably too busy watching TV and listening to some announcer tell you which brand of toothpaste to buy or how bad the economy is.

Listen to me. The Holy Spirit isn't going to be able to get through to you while you're lying around watching television. He's a gentleman. He just isn't going to come, grab the remote control out of your hand, and say, "Listen to Me, dummy! I have some important things to tell you."

No. He'll wait quietly for you to shut off all that other junk that's been occupying your mind and tune in to Him.

Right here is where most believers miss it. They're so involved in life, and even so involved in church activities and religious organizations that they don't ever have any time to spend with the Lord. They never just stop and fellowship with Him. All He gets is a few moments with them as they drive down the freeway or a few minutes between television commercials, and most of that is filled with "poor ol' me."

There are believers God has wanted to put into high political offices. He would have shown them how to solve some of their nation's problems. But He couldn't get their attention. So He just left them where they were, spinning their wheels in a dead-end job. There are others God would have promoted until they became chief executives of major corporations, but they were too busy working toward their own little goals to find out what His goals were.

Don't miss out on God's plans of prosperity for you. Spend time with Him. Listen to Him and learn to recognize His voice.

It's going to take more than a couple of Bible verses and a five-minute prayer to tap into the revelations the Holy Spirit has for you. You'll have to get serious about it.

If you think you don't have time to do that, think again.

How many hours a day do you spend in front of the television? How many hours a week do you spend reading the newspaper? How many hours reading novels and looking at magazines? How much time thinking about your problems?

Replace those things with the Word of God. Use that time to meditate on the Scriptures. Get in prayer and say, "Holy Spirit, I need to know what to do regarding this situation I'm in." Then listen. He'll start giving you the wisdom of God concerning your finances (or any other part of your life).

Will He really? Sure He will. James 1:5-6 says: *"If any of you lack wisdom, let him ask of God, that giveth to all men liberally, and upbraideth not; and it shall be given him. But let him ask in faith, nothing wavering. For he that wavereth is like a wave of the sea driven with the wind and tossed."*

Again, though, let me warn you. We're talking about more than reading a few quick scriptures a day and wishing for prosperity. We're talking about digging into the Word and staying there until you begin to hear from the Holy Spirit and until you develop a faith that doesn't waver.

That's not something that happens overnight. Like a spiritual farmer, you must plant and weed and water the Word within you. It will take some time and some work, but believe me, the harvest will be well worth the effort.

Heaven's Economics: "Laws of Abundance"

Chapter 16

"But my God shall supply all your need according to his riches in glory by Christ Jesus."
— PHILIPPIANS 4:19

Kenneth
Copeland

If, in spite of all the Bible's promises about prosperity...in spite of all the prayers you've prayed...you are still struggling financially today, I want you to consider this question: Where do you think God is going to get the resources to meet your needs?

Without even realizing it, many believers limit God because they have their eyes trained on the limited resources of this world rather than the unlimited riches of God's kingdom. Their faith fails when they think of the troubled economy on the earth, of the shortages and the scarcity that surrounds them. They wonder, *How is God going to bless me in the middle of all this?*

If that's what you've been thinking, here's some news that will turn those thoughts around!

The Bible says in Colossians 1:13 that God has *"delivered us from the power of darkness, and hath translated us into the kingdom of his dear Son."* To be translated means to be taken out of one place and put over into another. In other words, your citizenship is not primarily of this earth. You are not primarily American or Canadian or Australian—you are first and foremost a citizen of the kingdom of God.

That means this planet doesn't have any right to dictate to you whether your needs are met or not. The Bible says God will meet your needs according to His riches in glory! (Philippians 4:19). You need to learn to live by heaven's economy, not earth's economy—and in heaven there is always more than enough.

A friend of mine was born and raised in Eastern Europe about the time of World War II. For years all he and his family knew were persecution and scarcity. They lived on the run, first from the Germans, then from the communists. They ate out of trash cans until they were finally caught and sent to a concentration camp.

Finally through some miracles of God and the prayers of a couple of grandmothers, they were able to get away and come to the United States. The first place they went when they got to this country was a grocery store. Can you imagine what it was like coming out of a concentration camp and going into a grocery store? They just walked up and down the aisles of that store and wept for joy at the abundance that was available.

If you and I would only wake up to the abundance of heaven that's been made available to us, that's how we'd feel too. We'd realize we've been translated out of the world of poverty into a kingdom that flows with milk and honey.

You know, God meant for us to come to that realization every time we tithe. He meant for us to give our tithe as a way of activating heaven's economy in our lives, to give it in gratitude and faith expecting our needs to be met abundantly.

In Deuteronomy 26, God told the Israelites exactly what to say when they brought their tithes. He instructed them to acknowledge the fact that He had brought them out of the bondage of Egypt and to say: *"The Lord brought us forth out of Egypt with a mighty hand, and with an outstretched arm, and with great terribleness, and with signs, and with wonders: And he hath brought us into this place, and hath given us this land, even a land that floweth with milk and honey"* (verses 8-9).

Hallelujah, God has done the same thing for us! So when you bring your tithe to the Lord, make it a time of rejoicing. Make it a time of realizing anew that you've been translated from a world of scarcity to a heavenly economy of abundance!

Here's a prayer to help you get started.

"Father, I thank You and praise You for translating me from the kingdom of darkness into the kingdom that You have prepared for me. Thank You that it is a kingdom of mercy, a kingdom of joy, a kingdom of peace, and a kingdom of abundance.

"I bring my tithe now to You, Lord Jesus. It is the firstfruits of what You have given me, and I plant it in Your kingdom as a seed of blessing, expecting the rich blessings of heaven to be multiplied to me in return.

"I thank You, Lord, that You've rebuked Satan for my sake, and I stand in agreement with Your Word that he'll not destroy my land. He'll not destroy my blessings, and he'll not destroy my crop in the field. I am a citizen of Your kingdom. I have the rights and privileges of a citizen of that kingdom, and I stand upon them. Thank You, Jesus, that heaven's unlimited resources are mine in Your Name! Amen."

Chapter 17

The Seeds of Your Success

> "Except a corn of wheat fall into the ground and die, it abideth alone: but if it die, it bringeth forth much fruit."
> — JOHN 12:24

Jerry Savelle

Some time ago I was scheduled to fly to Tulsa, Okla., to speak in a meeting. Before I left home, I tried to talk to the Lord about some critical needs in my life and ministry. Instead of answering the way I had expected, He told me, *When you get to Tulsa, I want you to give away your van.* I dropped the subject.

On the plane I again approached the Lord about my pressing situation. "Father, I really need to talk to You about my needs," I told Him. "It just seems they have become overwhelming."

Again, the Lord spoke to me and said, *When you get to Tulsa, I want you to give away your van.* So again, I dropped the subject.

A while later, I once more took up my "case" with the Lord: "Father, during this meeting in Tulsa, I am going to have a little time between services, and I really need to talk to You about my needs."

Once more there came His response, *When you get to Tulsa, I want you to give away your van.* But this time He went on: *Also, there are five preachers in Tulsa who have become discouraged and are about to give up the ministry. I want you to give each of them a suit of clothes.* So once more I decided not to continue the discussion.

Finally, I just couldn't hold back any longer. I said to the Lord, "Father, I've just got to talk to You! You know we've been building our international headquarters in Fort Worth this year. We have moved into them, but there are still lots of things we need. More land, for instance, and more buildings. But we just don't have the money to get what we need...."

When you get to Tulsa, I want you to give away your van and five suits of clothes.

It was then that it finally hit me what was happening. Every time I tried to talk to God about my need, He talked to me about seed.

Now, that's not deep. As children of God, all of us should understand it. We are seed-planting people. But, if you are like me, you have probably noticed that over the past couple of years, your needs have grown larger and larger. You must be wondering, as I was on that plane, where in the world the money is going to come from to meet those steadily increasing obligations.

I believe the Lord showed me the answer to that important question while I was in that airplane on my way to Tulsa. He told me, *In the days to come, the needs of the Body of Christ are going to become so great that, in the natural, they will appear to be impossible to meet. But I am telling you now, don't wait until then to get busy sowing seed into the kingdom.... Don't wait until you get an answer to your present needs before you begin to prepare for the future needs.*

213

Then He made a statement that suddenly put the whole subject into perspective for me:

You must become seed-conscious, not need-conscious.

That's how God Himself is—He's seed-conscious. When He had "needs" of His own, He fulfilled those needs by giving. He "needed" the redemption of mankind. He "needed" a family. So what did He do? He planted a seed. He gave Jesus.

Our Lord told us plainly: *"Except a corn of wheat fall into the ground and die, it abideth alone: but if it die, it bringeth forth much fruit"* (John 12:24). God sowed His "Seed," His only Son Jesus, into the earth and reaped in return a harvest of sons and daughters. He planted the best seed heaven had to offer, not worthless seed. He didn't look for some old decrepit, worn-out angel to use as seed, someone who was no longer needed. No, He chose and planted the very best He had. And He reaped the best of all harvests—human souls.

God explains that principle of seed planting and harvest clearly in Ecclesiastes 11:1-6. There He says:

> Give generously, for your gifts will return to you later. Divide your gifts among many, for in the days ahead you yourself may need much help. When the clouds are heavy, the rains come down; when a tree falls, whether south or north, the die is cast, for there it lies. If you wait for perfect conditions, you will never get anything done. God's ways are as mysterious as the pathway of the wind and as the manner in which a human spirit is infused into the little body of a baby while it is yet in its mother's womb. Keep on sowing your seed, for you never know which will grow—perhaps it all will *(The Living Bible)*.

Now, in this passage we see a vital principle of godly giving: *"Give generously, for your gifts will return to you later."*

You might say to me, "I just don't understand that. I don't understand how I can give away something and expect God to give it back to me."

I know you don't understand it. Neither do I. It is not necessary that we understand God's principles to benefit from them. We must simply learn then, believe them, and act upon them.

For example, we don't know how seeds bring forth plants for fruit. We just know they do, so we sow seeds into the ground, patiently tend and nurture them, and then reap an abundant harvest from them. That's what God expects us to do with the good seed of His Word.

It is our job to sow seeds, God's job to meet needs.

But notice that the Bible says only that our godly gifts will come back to us. It doesn't say how or when. I wish I could tell you how and when your gift will be returned to you in multiplied form. I don't know. But I do know one thing: The time between sowing and reaping is the most important and exciting in our lives. It becomes a great adventure in faith. The secret is to sow faithfully, generously, and regularly so that we can expect a continual flow of godly gifts in return.

When my staff and I first began our ministry in Africa, we had to go through a battle royal in that land. At every step we had to battle corruption and opposition. But God had told us to go into that area and pull down the strongholds of Satan, and that was exactly what we intended to do, troubles or no troubles.

Our loyal workers lived under constant threat, in turmoil and stress 24 hours a day, with never a moment to relax. They were never able to let down their guard for an instant. The warfare they were engaged in was not only spiritual, but also natural. Some people were so opposed to the ministry, they had actually hired assassins to kill the members of our staff.

But despite the dangers, obstacles, and opposition from both man and Satan, we just kept on planting seeds into that outreach, week after week, month after month. After nine long months of seeming failure, we finally began to see a return on our investment in those precious African lives. Now my staff there can hardly contain their joy because every day brings a new victory over the forces of evil and darkness. All the seed we had been faithfully and consistently planting suddenly began to grow and produce fruit for the kingdom of God.

So don't become discouraged and quit sowing. Don't stop planting seed just because you don't see any immediate results. Keep sowing.

Prayer for Salvation and Baptism in the Holy Spirit

Heavenly Father, I come to You in the Name of Jesus. Your Word says, *"Whosoever shall call on the name of the Lord shall be saved"* (Acts 2:21), so I am calling on You. I pray and ask Jesus to come into my heart and be Lord over my life, according to Romans 10:9—*"If thou shalt confess with thy mouth the Lord Jesus, and shalt believe in thine heart that God hath raised him from the dead, thou shalt be saved."* I do that now. I confess that Jesus is Lord, and I believe in my heart that God raised Him from the dead. I am now reborn! I am a Christian—a child of Almighty God! I am saved!

You also said in Your Word, *"If ye then, being evil, know how to give good gifts unto your children: HOW MUCH MORE shall your heavenly Father give the Holy Spirit to them that ask him?"* (Luke 11:13). I'm also asking You to fill me with the Holy Spirit. Holy Spirit, rise up within me as I praise God. I fully expect to speak with other tongues as You give me utterance (Acts 2:4).

Now begin to praise God for filling you with the Holy Spirit. Speak those words and syllables you receive—not in your own language, but in the one given you by the Holy Spirit. You have to use your own voice because God will not force you to speak. Worship and praise Him in your heavenly language—in other tongues.

Continue with the blessing God has given you and pray in tongues each day.

You are a born-again, Spirit-filled believer. You'll never be the same!

Find a good Word of God preaching church, and become a part of a church family who will love and care for you as you love and care for them.

We need to be hooked up to each other. It increases our strength in God. It's God's plan for us.

About the Authors

As founders of Kenneth Copeland Ministries in Fort Worth, Texas, Kenneth and Gloria circle the globe with the uncompromised Word of God, preaching and teaching a lifestyle of victory for every Christian. They are committed to reaching entire families—grandparents, parents, young men and women and children.

Their daily and Sunday *Believer's Voice of Victory* television broadcast now airs on more than 500 stations around the world and their BVOV and *Shout!* magazines are distributed to one million adults and children worldwide. Their international prison ministry reaches an average of 60,000 new inmates every year and receives more than 17,000 pieces of correspondence each month. With offices and staff in the United States, Canada, England, Australia, South Africa and Ukraine, Kenneth and Gloria's teaching materials—books, magazines, audios and videos—have been into at least 22 languages to reach the world with the love of God.

Books Available From
Kenneth Copeland Publications

by Kenneth Copeland

* A Ceremony of Marriage
  A Matter of Choice
  Covenant of Blood
  Faith and Patience—The Power Twins
* Freedom From Fear
  Giving and Receiving
  Honor—Walking in Honesty, Truth and Integrity
  How to Conquer Strife
  How to Discipline Your Flesh
  How to Receive Communion
  Living at the End of Time—A Time of Supernatural Increase
  Love Never Fails
  Managing God's Mutual Funds
* Now Are We in Christ Jesus
* Our Covenant With God
* Prayer—Your Foundation for Success
  Prosperity: The Choice Is Yours
  Rumors of War
* Sensitivity of Heart
  Six Steps to Excellence in Ministry
  Sorrow Not! Winning Over Grief and Sorrow
* The Decision Is Yours
* The Force of Faith
* The Force of Righteousness
  The Image of God in You
  The Laws of Prosperity
* The Mercy of God
  The Miraculous Realm of God's Love
  The Outpouring of the Spirit—The Result of Prayer
* The Power of the Tongue
  The Power to Be Forever Free
  The Troublemaker
* The Winning Attitude
  Turn Your Hurts Into Harvests
* Welcome to the Family
* You Are Healed!
  Your Right-Standing With God

by Gloria Copeland

* And Jesus Healed Them All
  Are You Ready?
  Build Your Financial Foundation
  Build Yourself an Ark
  Fight On!
  God's Prescription for Divine Health
  God's Success Formula
  God's Will for You
  God's Will for Your Healing

God's Will is Prosperity
* God's Will Is the Holy Spirit
* Harvest of Health
Hidden Treasures
Living Contact
* Love—The Secret to Your Success
No Deposit—No Return
Pleasing the Father
Pressing In—It's Worth It All
The Power to Live a New Life
The Unbeatable Spirit of Faith
* Walk in the Spirit
Walk With God
Well Worth the Wait

Books Co-Authored by Kenneth and Gloria Copeland

Family Promises
Healing Promises
Prosperity Promises

From Faith to Faith—A Daily Guide to Victory
One Word From God Series
• One Word from God Can Change Your Destiny
• One Word from God Can Change Your Family
• One Word from God Can Change Your Finances
• One Word from God Can Change Your Health
Over the Edge—A Youth Devotional
Over the Edge Xtreme Planner for Students
Pursuit of His Presence—A Daily Devotional
Pursuit of His Presence—A Perpetual Calendar

Other Books Published by KCP

The First 30 Years—A Journey of Faith
    The story of the lives of Kenneth and Gloria Copeland
Real People. Real Needs. Real Victories.
    A book of testimonies to encourage your faith.

John G. Lake—His Life, His Sermons, His Boldness of Faith

The Holiest of All, by Andrew Murray
The New Testament in Modern Speech, by
    Richard Francis Weymouth

Products Designed by KCP and Heirborne™
for Today's Children and Youth

Baby Praise Board Book
Best of *Shout!* Adventure Comics
Noah's Ark Coloring Book
Shout! Super-Activity Book
Superkid Novels
• Escape from Jungle Island
• In Pursuit of the Enemy
• Mysterious Presence, The
• Quest for the Second Half, The
SWORD Adventure Book

*Available in Spanish

World Offices of
Kenneth Copeland Ministries

For more information about KCM and a free
catalog, please write the office nearest you:

Kenneth Copeland Ministries
Fort Worth, Texas 76192-0001

Kenneth Copeland Ministries
Locked Bag 2600
Mansfield Delivery Centre
QUEENSLAND 4122
AUSTRALIA

Kenneth Copeland Ministries
Post Office Box 15
BATH
BA1 1GD
ENGLAND

Kenneth Copeland Ministries
Private Bag X 909
FONTAINEBLEAU
2032
REPUBLIC OF
   SOUTH AFRICA

Kenneth Copeland Ministries
Post Office Box 378
Surrey
BRITISH COLUMBIA
V3T 5B6
CANADA

UKRAINE
L'VIV 290000
Post Office Box 84
Kenneth Copeland Ministries
L'VIV 290000
UKRAINE

Learn more about Kenneth Copeland Ministries
by visiting our website at:
www.kcm.org

Believer's Voice of Victory

Enjoy inspired teaching and encouragement from Kenneth and Gloria Copeland and guest ministers each month in the *Believers Voice of Victory* magazine. Also included are real-life testimonies of God's miraculous power and divine intervention into the lives of people just like you! It's more than just a magazine—it's a ministry.

S H O U T!

...the dynamic magazine just for kids!

Shout! The Voice of Victory for Kids is a Bible-charged, action-packed, bi-monthly magazine available FREE to kids everywhere!

Featuring *Wichita Slim* and *Commander Kellie and the Superkids, Shout!* is filled with colorful adventure comics, challenging games and puzzles, exciting short stories, solve-it-yourself mysteries and much more! Stand up, sign up and get ready to *Shout!*

If you or someone you know would like to receive a FREE subscription to *Shout!*, send each kid's name, date of birth and complete address to:

To receive a FREE subscription to *Believers Voice of Victory*, or to give a child you know a FREE subscription to *Shout!*, write:

Kenneth Copeland Ministries
Fort Worth, Texas 76192-0001
or call:
1-800-359-0075
(9 a.m.-5 p.m. CT)
Or visit our website at:
www.kcm.org

If you are writing from outside the U.S.,
please contact the KCM office nearest you.
Addresses for all Kenneth Copeland Ministries
offices are listed on the previous page.

We're Here for You!

Join Kenneth and Gloria Copeland, and the *Believer's Voice of Victory* broadcasts, Monday through Friday and on Sunday each week, and learn how faith in God's Word can take your life from ordinary to extraordinary. This teaching from God's Word is designed to get you where you want to be—on top!

You can catch the *Believer's Voice of Victory* broadcast on your local, cable or satellite channels:

Sunday
9-9:30 p.m. ET
Cable*/G5, Channel 3—TBN
INSP

Monday through Friday
6-6:30 a.m. ET
Cable*/G5, Channel 7—WGN
TBN

Monday through Friday
6:30-7 a.m. ET
Cable*/G5,
Channel 20—BET

Monday through Friday
7-7:30 p.m. ET
Cable*G1, Channel 17—

Monday through Friday
11-11:30 a.m. ET
Cable*G5, Channel 3—

Monday through Friday
10:30-11 a.m. CT
Cable*Spacenet 3,
Transponder 13-KMPX

*Check your local listings for more times and stations ir your area.

The Harrison House Vision

Proclaiming the truth and the power
Of the Gospel of Jesus Christ
With excellence;
Challenging Christians to
Live victoriously,
Grow spiritually,
Know God intimately.